Guelph Ontario Book 2 in Colour Photos, Saving Our History One Photo at a Time

Photography
by Barbara Raué
2014

Series Name:
Cruising Ontario

Book 86: Guelph

Cover photo: Ontario Veterinary College

Series Name: Cruising Ontario
Saving Our History One Photo at a Time

Other Books by Barbara Raue

Coins of Gold

Arrows, Indians and Love

The Life and Times of Barbara
Volume 1: Inventions That Have Enhanced My Life
Volume 2: Entertainment That I Have Enjoyed
Volume 3: East Coast Trips
Volume 4: Olympics Have Always Intrigued Me
Volume 5: Wonders of the World
Volume 6: Caribbean Cruises We Have Enjoyed
Volume 7: Animals
Volume 8: Storms and Other Major Disasters in My Lifetime
Volume 9: Wars, Terrorist Attacks and Major Disasters

The Cromwell Family Book

Laura Secord Discovered

Visit Barbara's website to view all of her books
http://barbararaue.ca

Guelph

Guelph, known as "The Royal City, is located 100 kilometers (62 miles) west of downtown Toronto at the intersection of Highways 6 and 7. Guelph was founded on St. George's Day, April 23, 1827, the feast day of the patron saint of England. The town was named to honour Britain's royal family, the Hanoverians who were descended from the Guelfs, the ancestral family of George IV, the reigning British monarch. The first cable TV system began in Guelph with their first broadcast being the coronation of Queen Elizabeth II in 1953. The Speed and Eramosa Rivers flow through the city.

The Ontario Agricultural College, the oldest part of the University of Guelph, began in 1873 as an associate agricultural college of the University of Toronto. The Government of Ontario purchased 550 acres of land from F. W. Stone to build the college. In 1964, the Ontario Agricultural College, Ontario Veterinary College and Macdonald Institute combined to become the University of Guelph and Wellington College.

Moffat

Moffat is located north of the 401, southeast of Guelph. We lived in Moffat from the fall of 1954 to the spring of 1956. Moffat was a small village with farms and a few homes on two side streets, a post office, general store, and a school.

We moved from Moffat to the outskirts of Guelph on Old York Road across from the Ontario Reformatory grounds. When the boundary of Guelph extended eastward, the name of our road became Beaumont Crescent and our house number was 18.

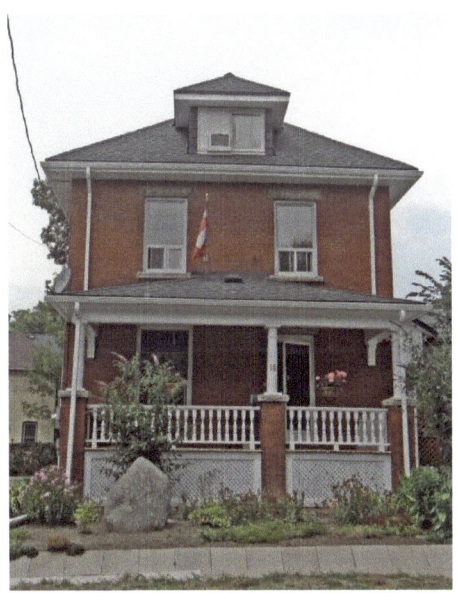

#14 – Italianate, dormer in attic

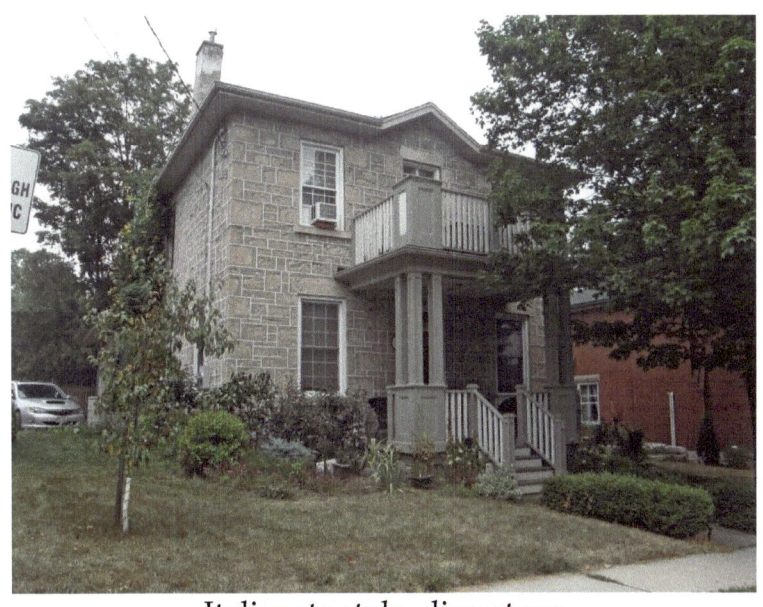

Italianate style - limestone

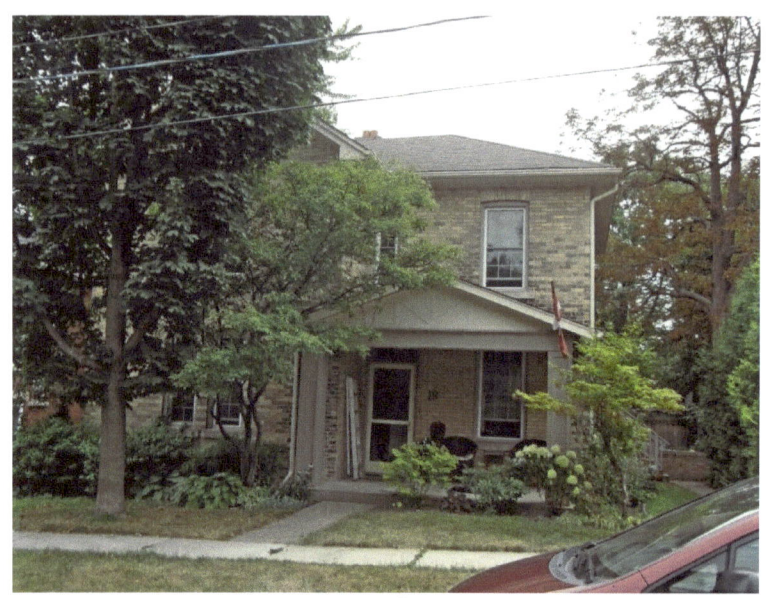

#19

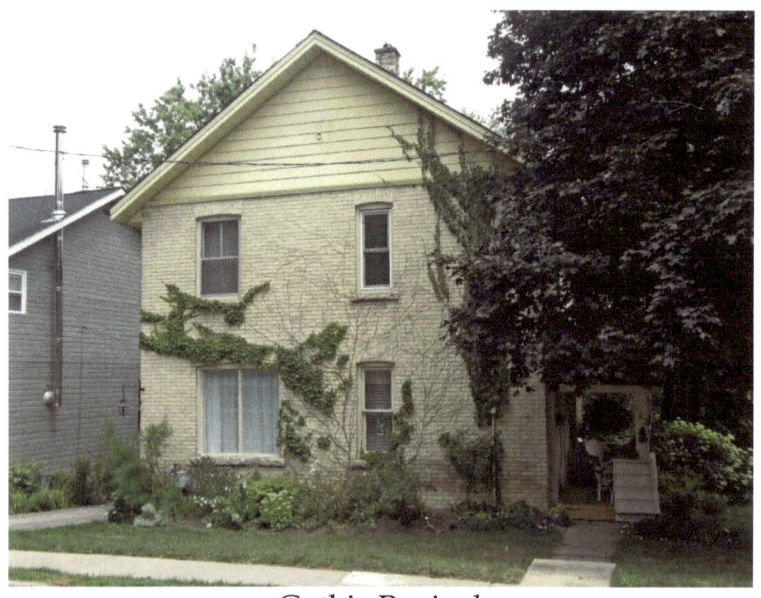

Gothic Revival

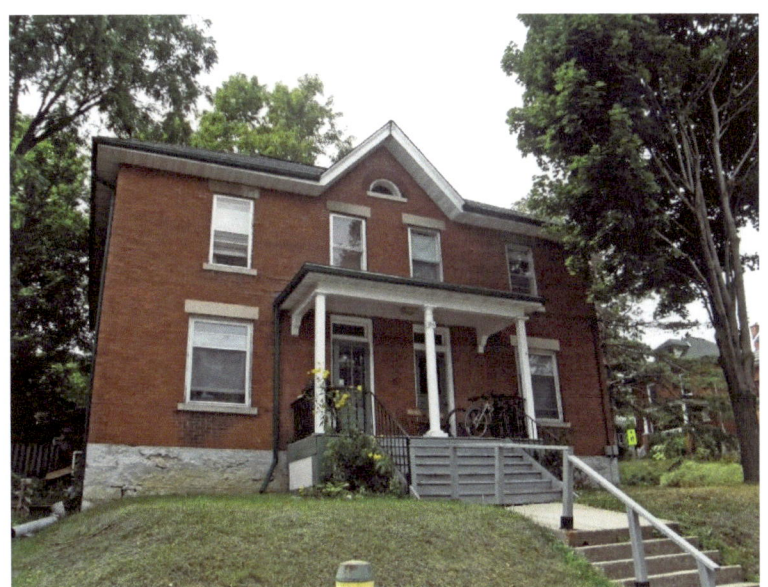

#116 – Italianate style, red brick

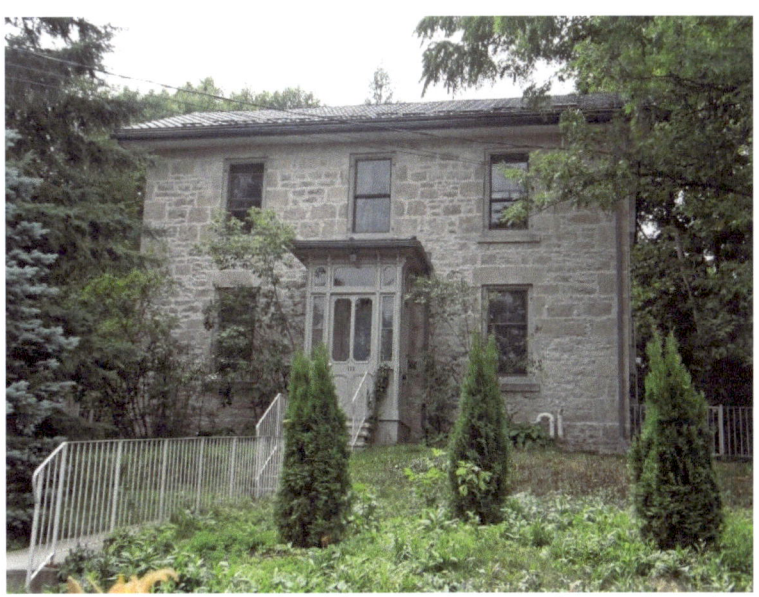

#112 - limestone building, Italianate, hipped roof

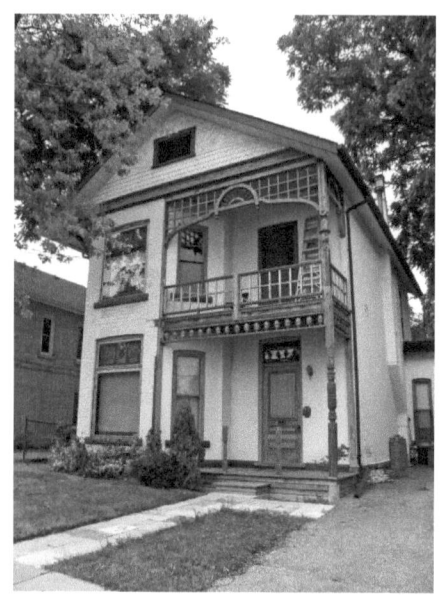

#6 – Gothic Revival

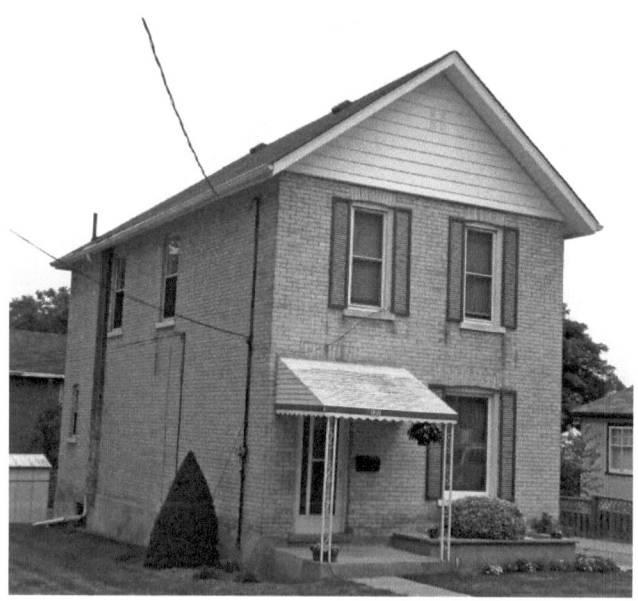

#101 – Gothic Revival – yellow brick

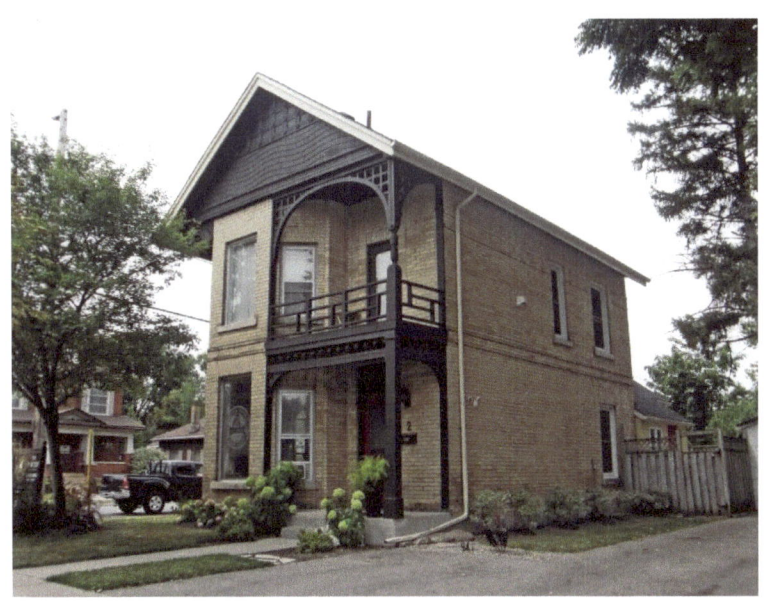

#2 – Gothic Revival – yellow brick

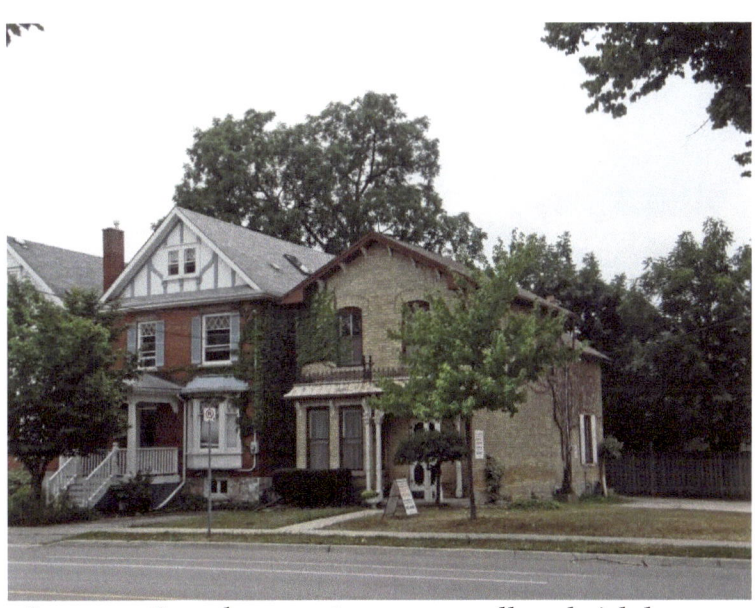

Iron cresting above entrance on yellow brick house;
Tudor style of red brick house, bay window

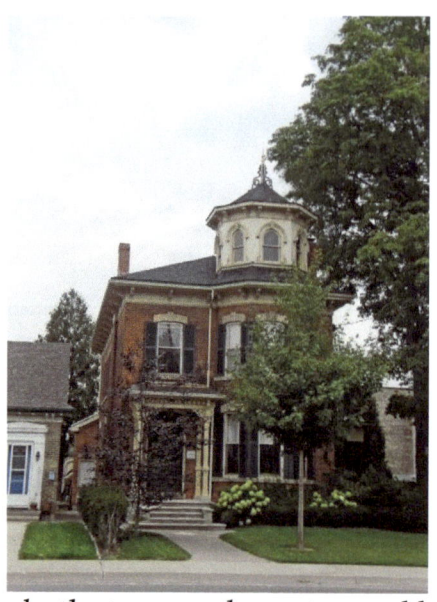

Bay windows on both storeys, plus octagonal belvedere on top

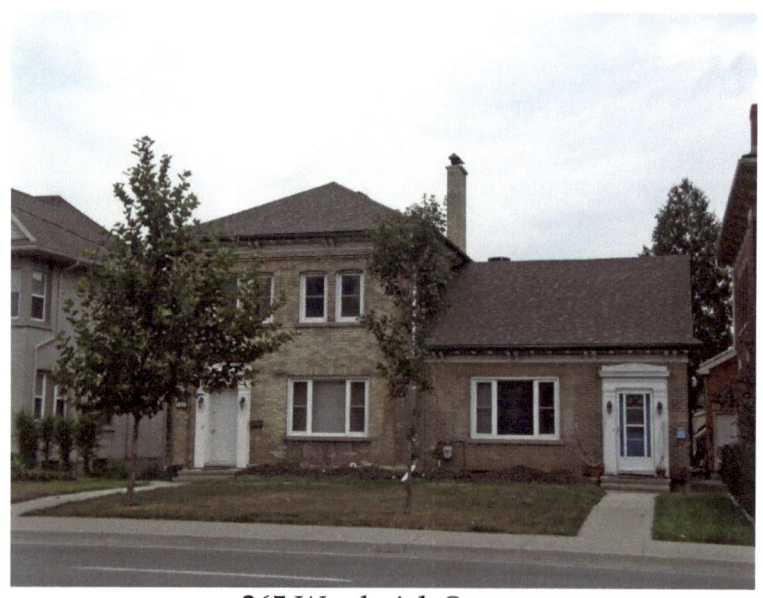

265 Woolwich Street

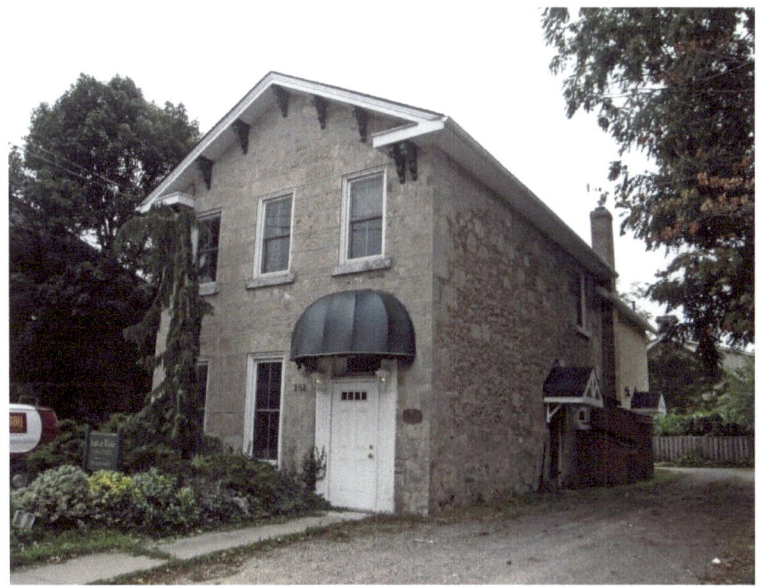

258 Woolwich Street – main stone portion built 1871-72
Single brackets, cornice return

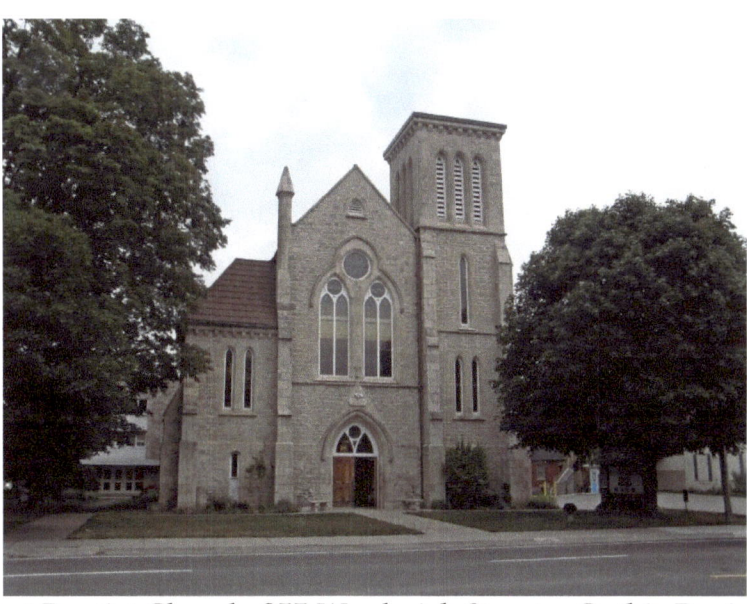

First Baptist Church, 255 Woolwich Street – Gothic Revival

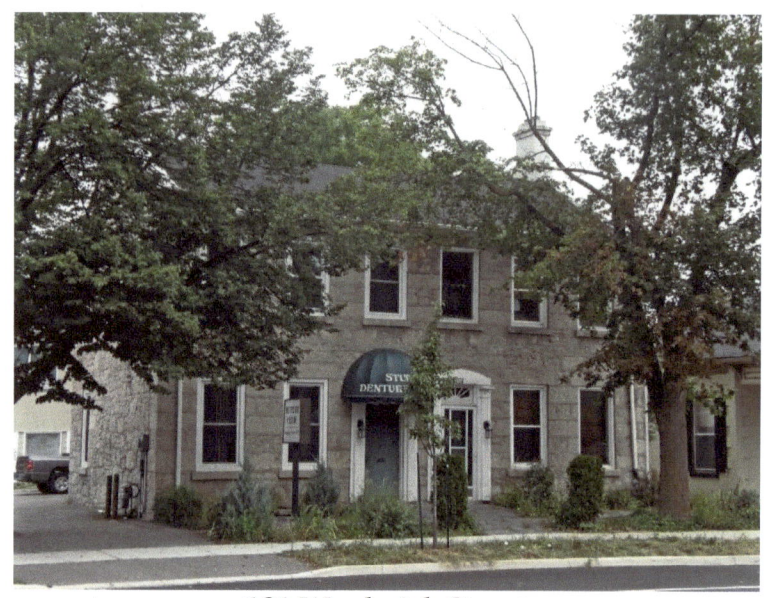

191 Woolwich Street

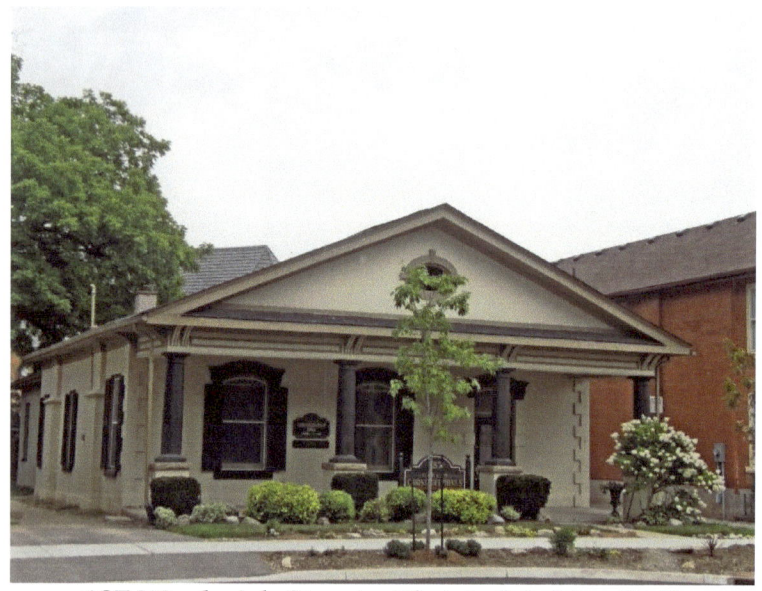

187 Woolwich Street - Christadelphian Hall

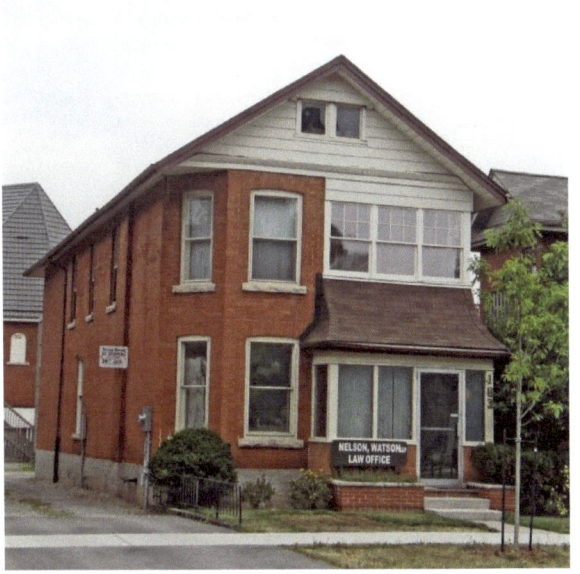

183 Woolwich Street - Edwardian

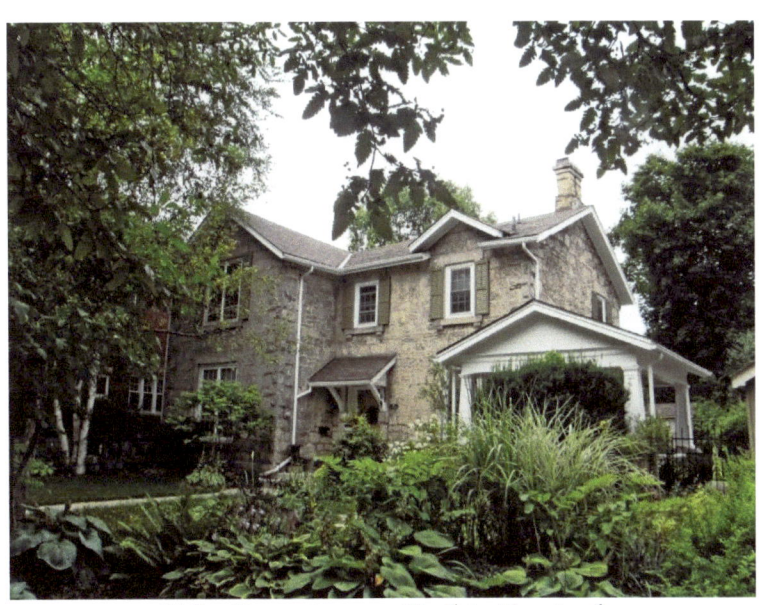

#15 – limestone – Gothic Revival,
cornice return on small gable

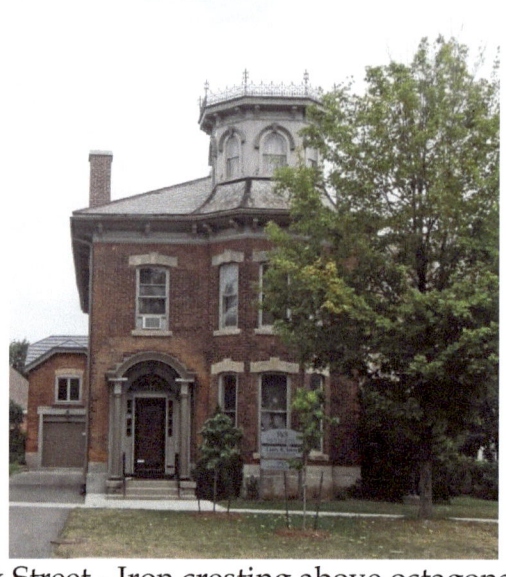

143 Norfolk Street - Iron cresting above octagonal belvedere

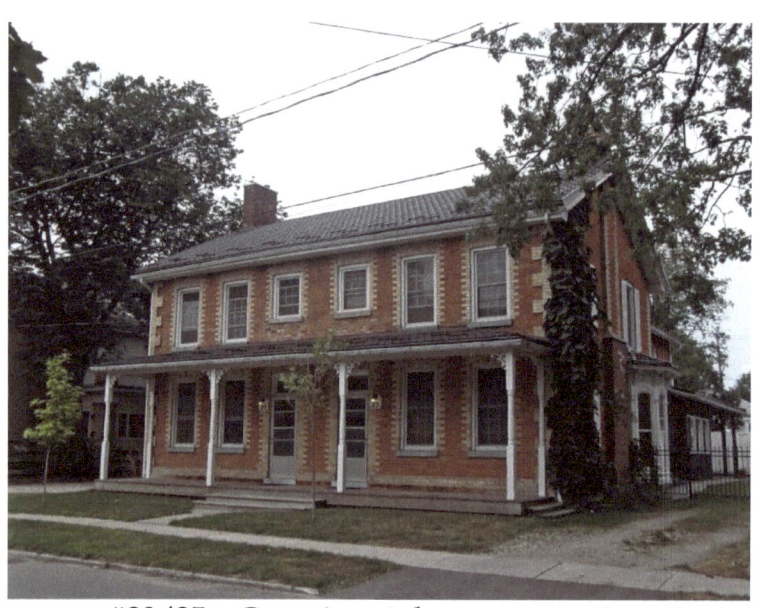

#23/25 – Georgian style, corner quoins,
Dichromatic brickwork

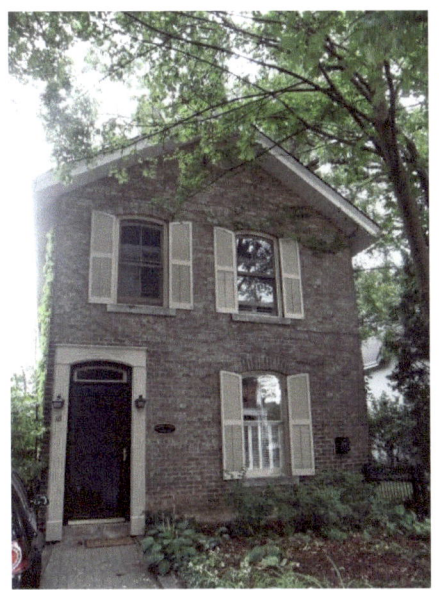

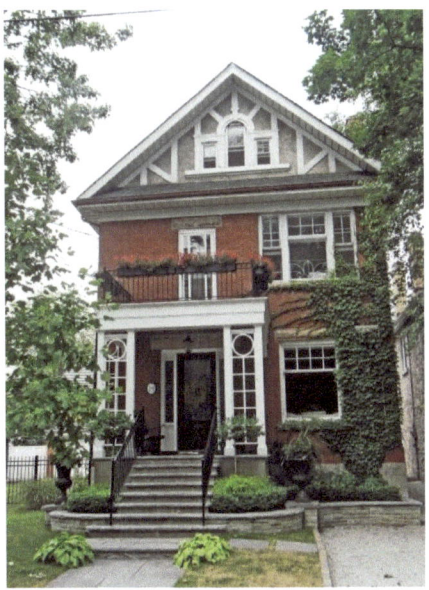

#18 – Donegal House circa 1867
Gothic Revival

#19 – Palladian window
Edwardian/Tudor style
Balcony on second floor

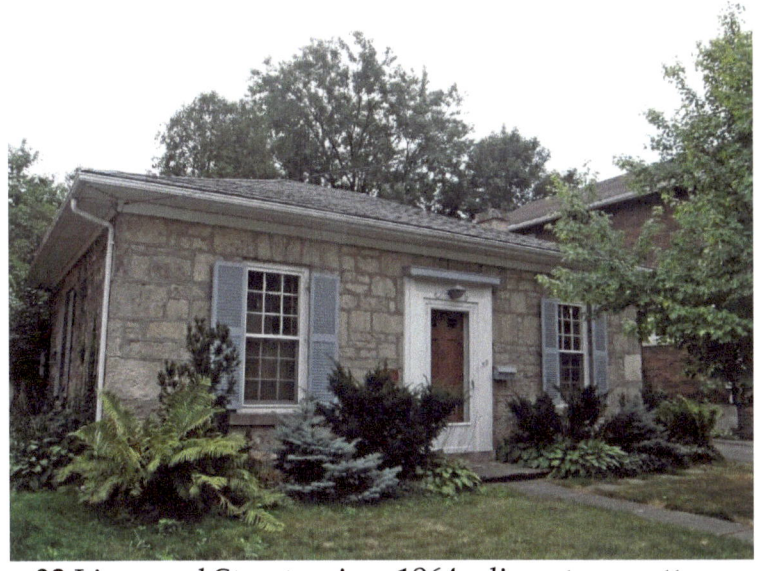

32 Liverpool Street – circa 1864 – limestone cottage

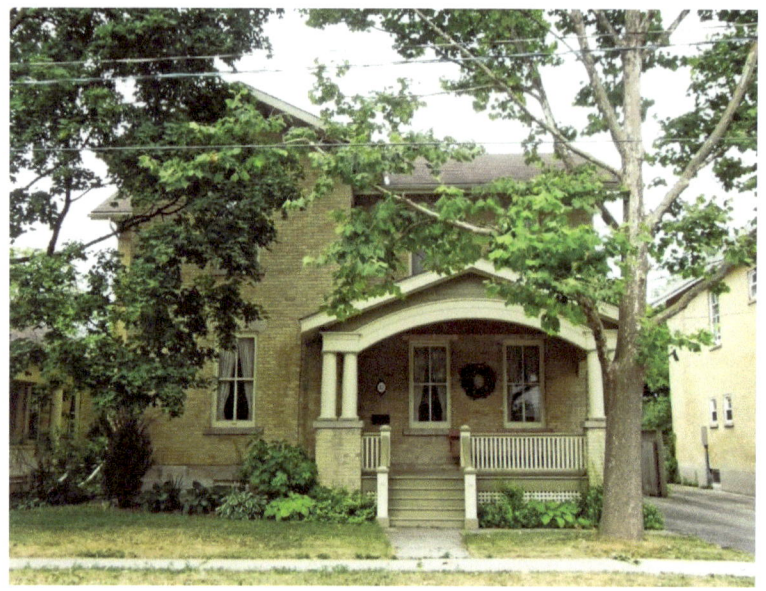

#37

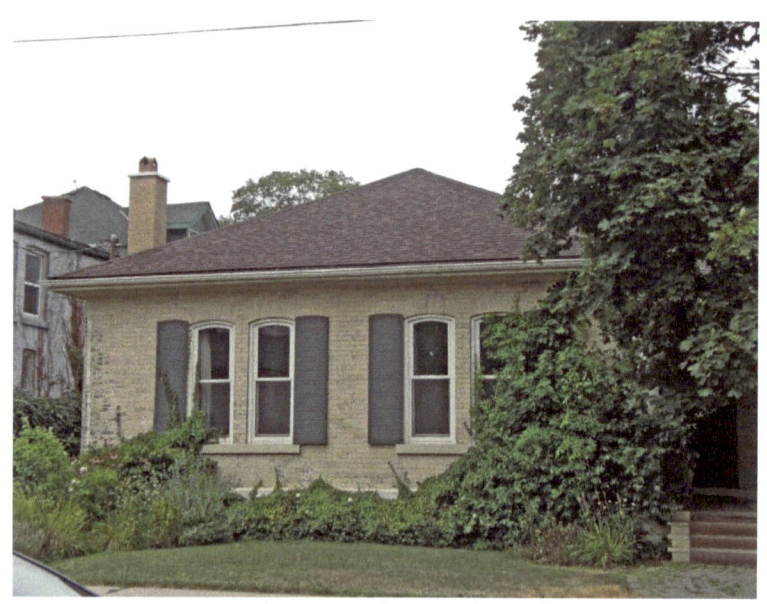

Italianate - hipped roof

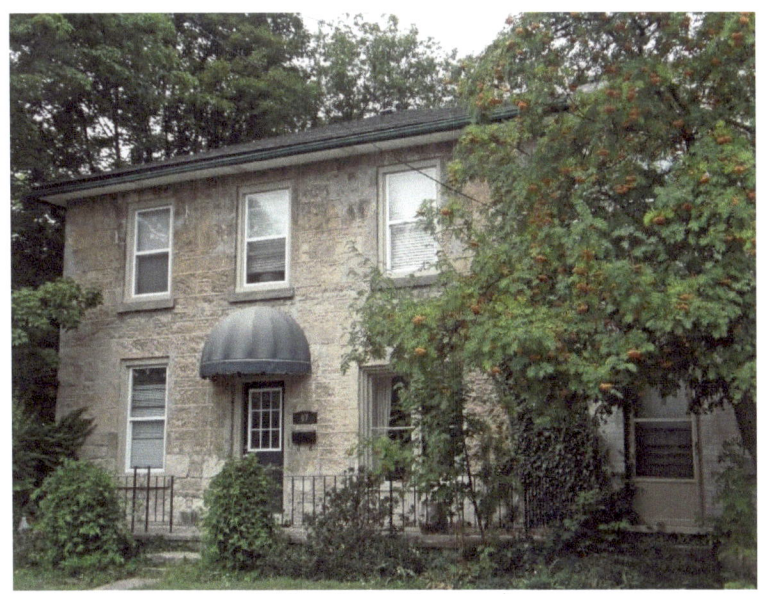

#47 – Georgian style

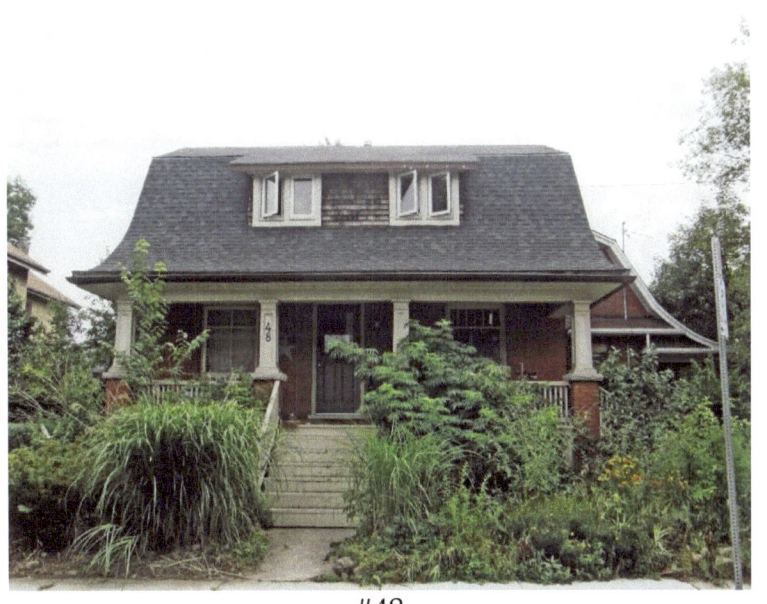

#48

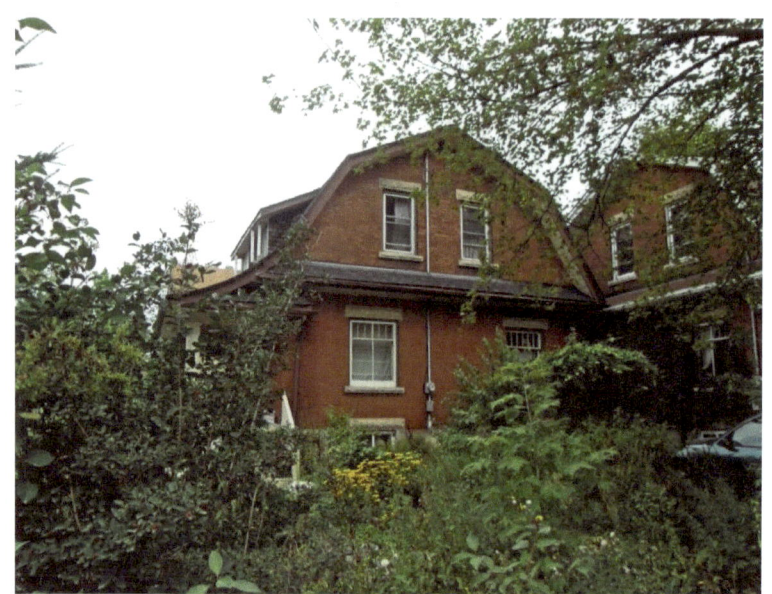

Red brick

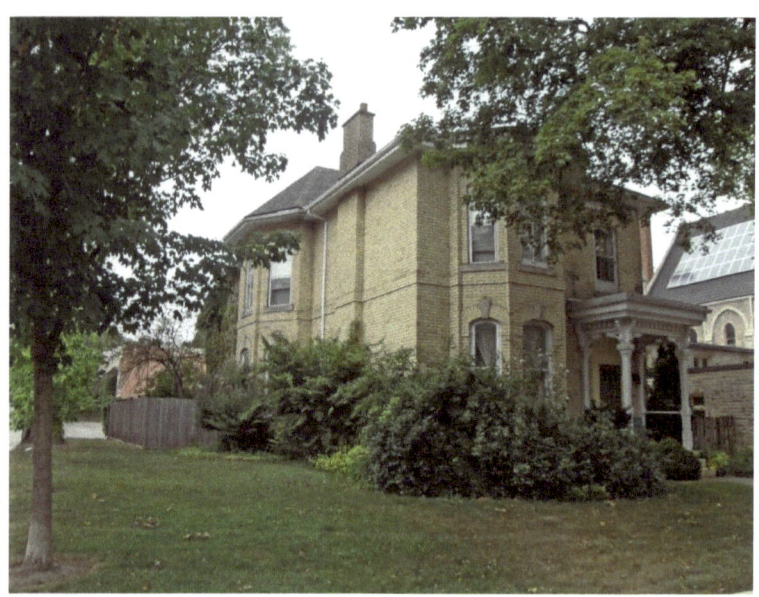

Yellow brick, two-storey bay window

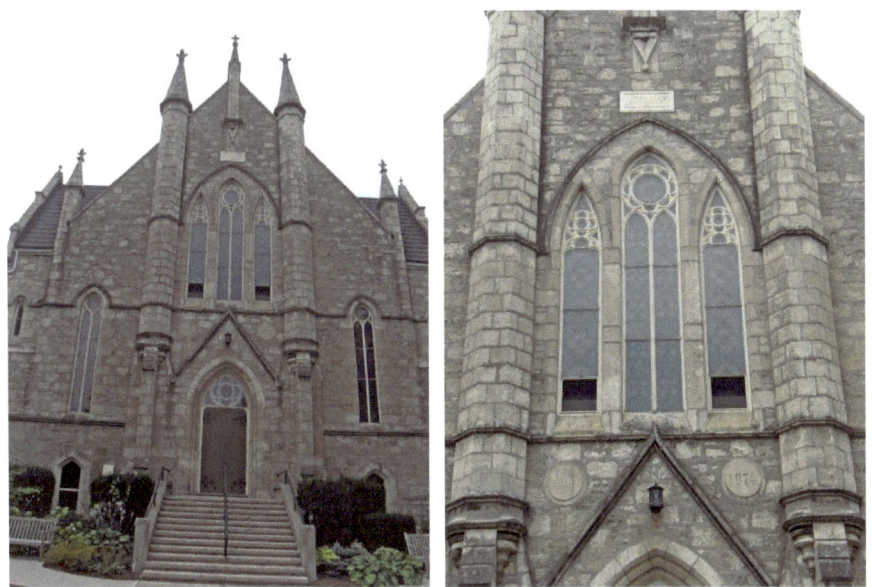

68 Suffolk Street West - Dublin Street United Church

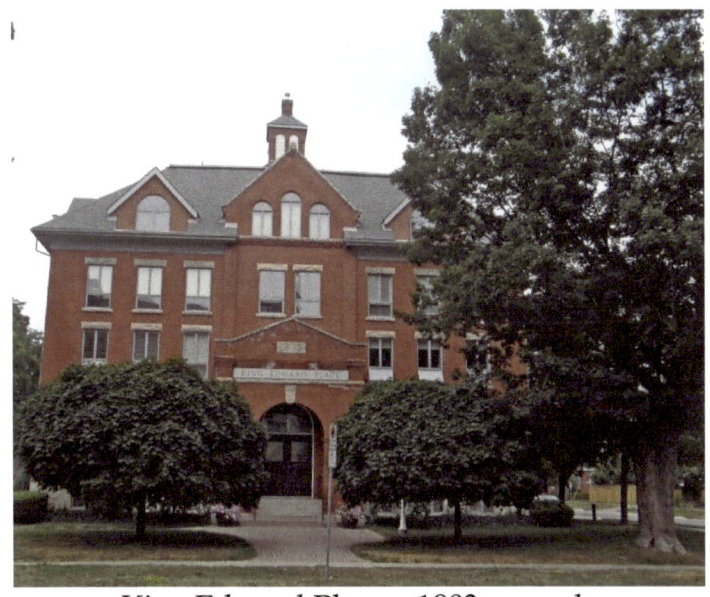

King Edward Place – 1903 - cupola

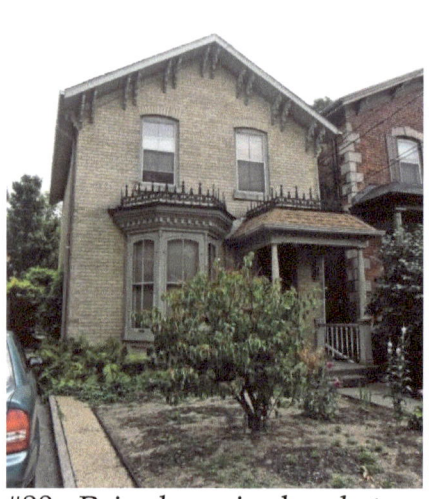

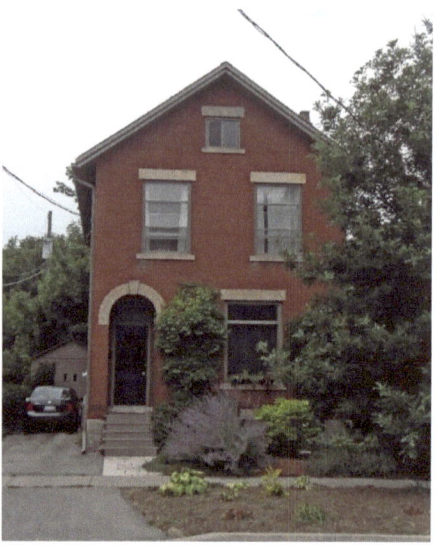

#80 - Paired cornice brackets, iron cresting above bay window and above entranceway

Gothic Revival arched voussoirs with keystones

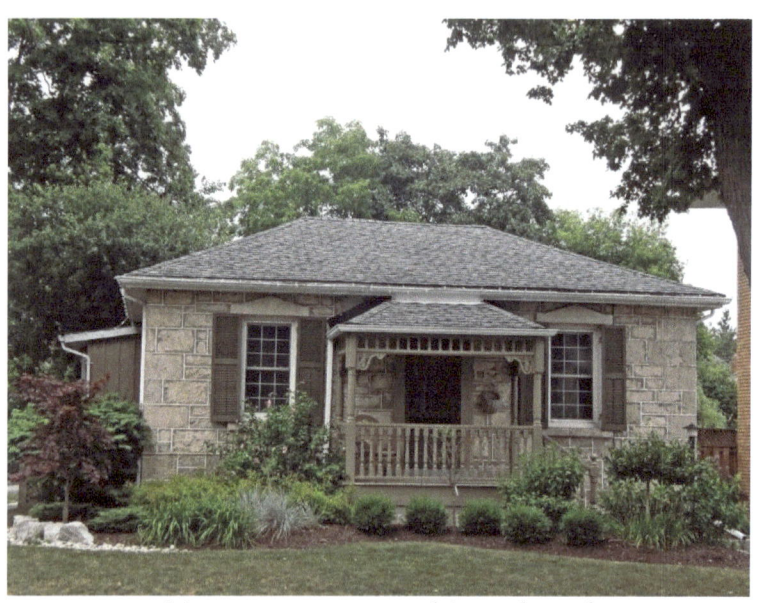

Limestone cottage, hipped roof

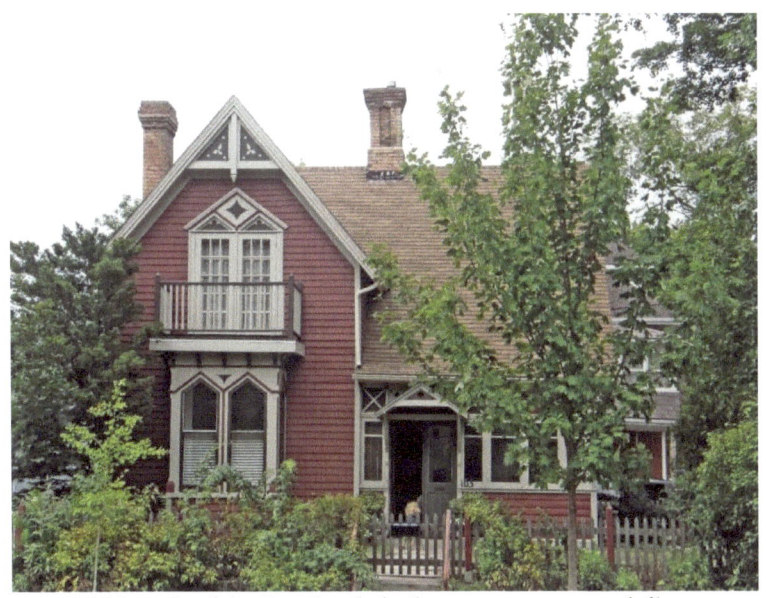

#103 – Gothic Revival, balcony on second floor

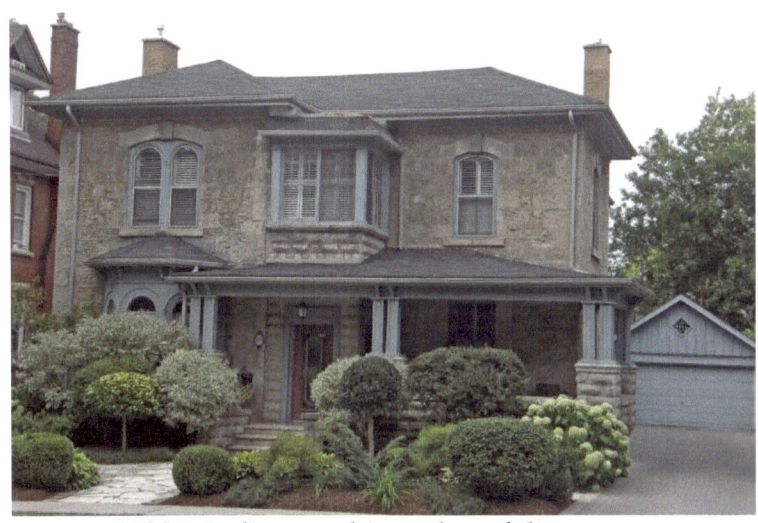

#109 – Italianate, hipped roof, limestone

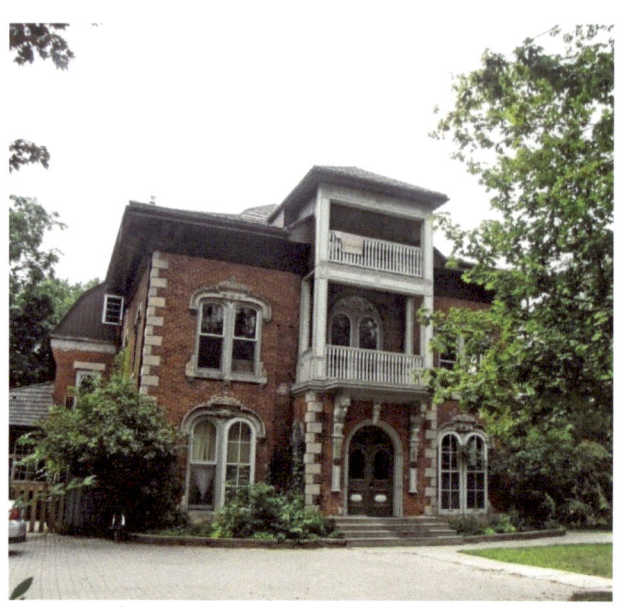

Corner quoins, decorative raised window hoods, balcony off second floor, and balcony off dormer in attic, with artistically decorated entranceway

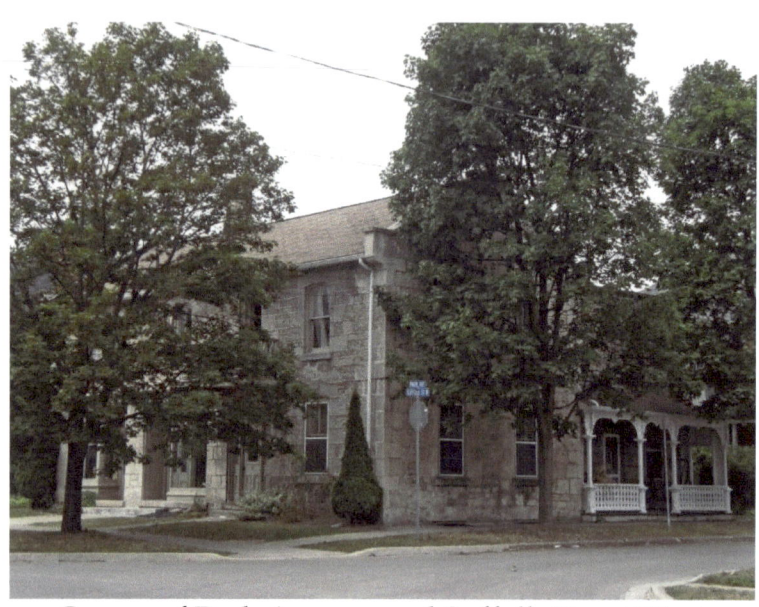

Corner of Park Avenue and Suffolk Street West

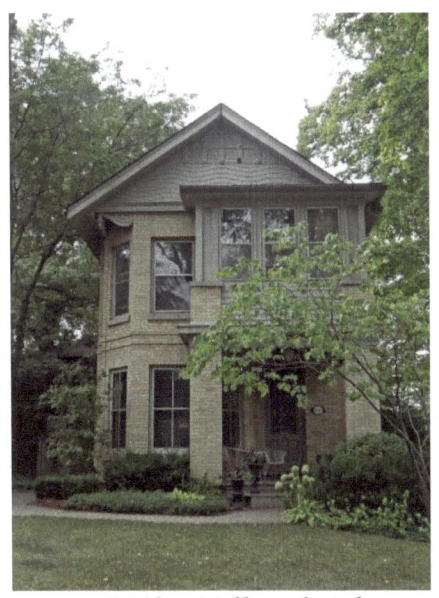
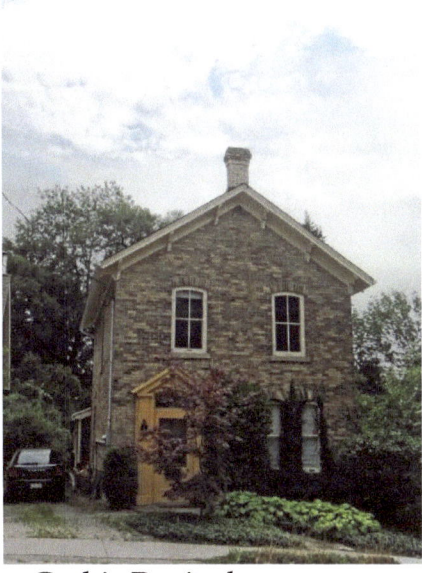

#160 – Yellow brick   Gothic Revival

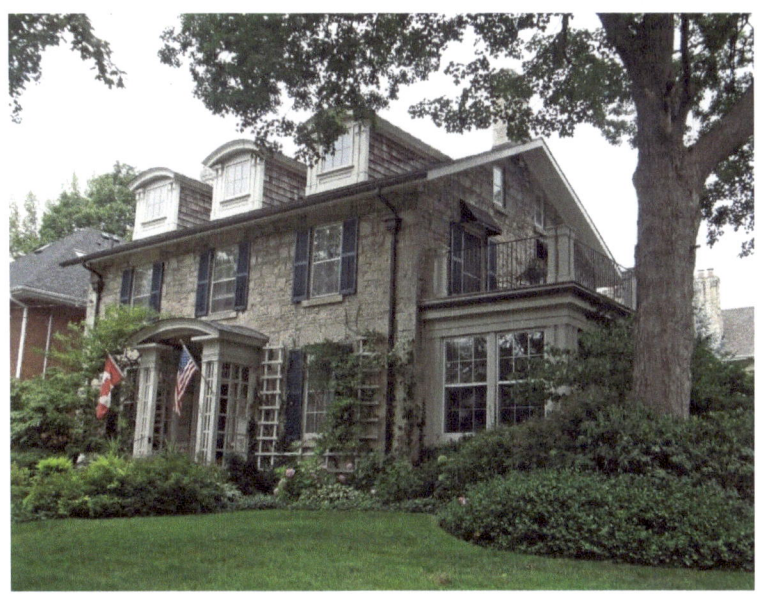

Limestone – Georgian style, dormers in attic, balcony off
second floor above enclosed sunroom

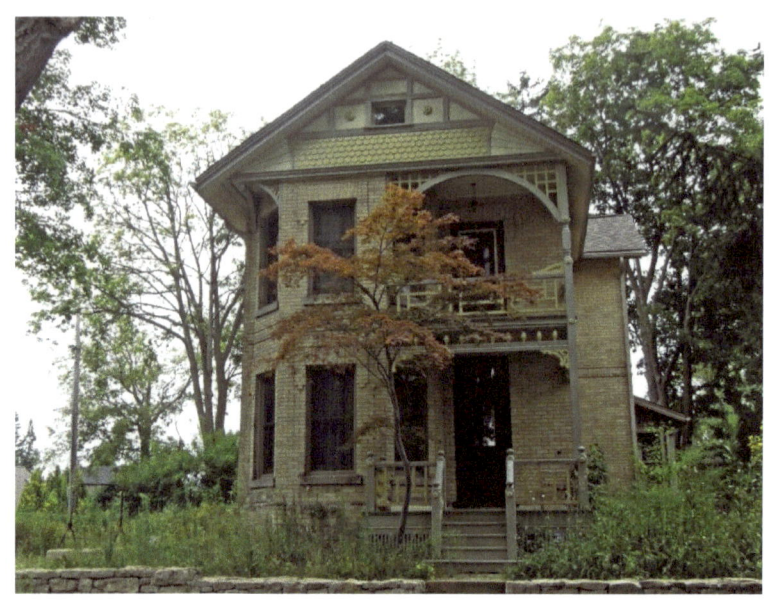

Gothic Revival

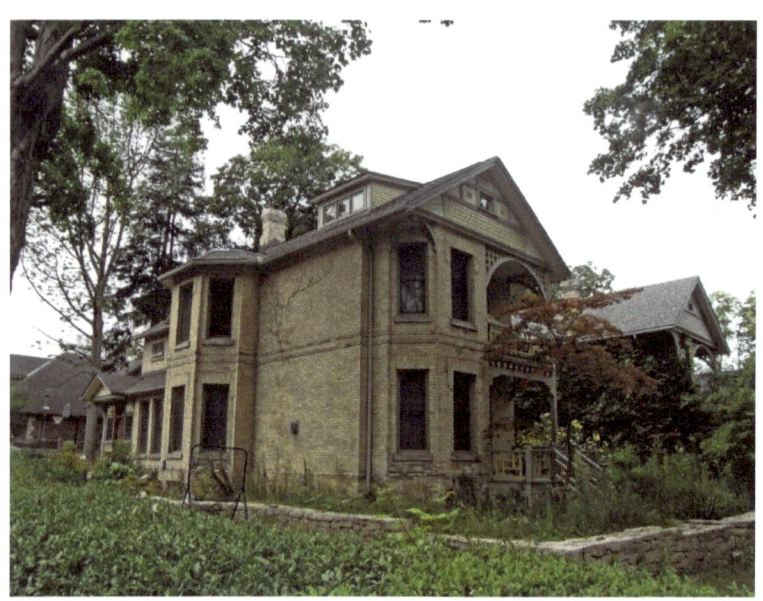

Balcony on second floor, two-storey bay window on side,
dormer in attic

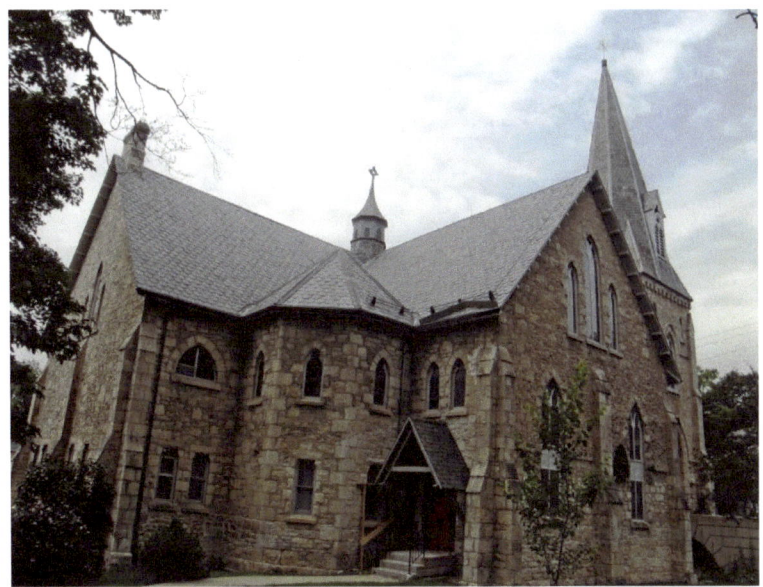

86 Glasgow Street North - St. James the Apostle Anglican
Church built of locally quarried limestone – 1891-92

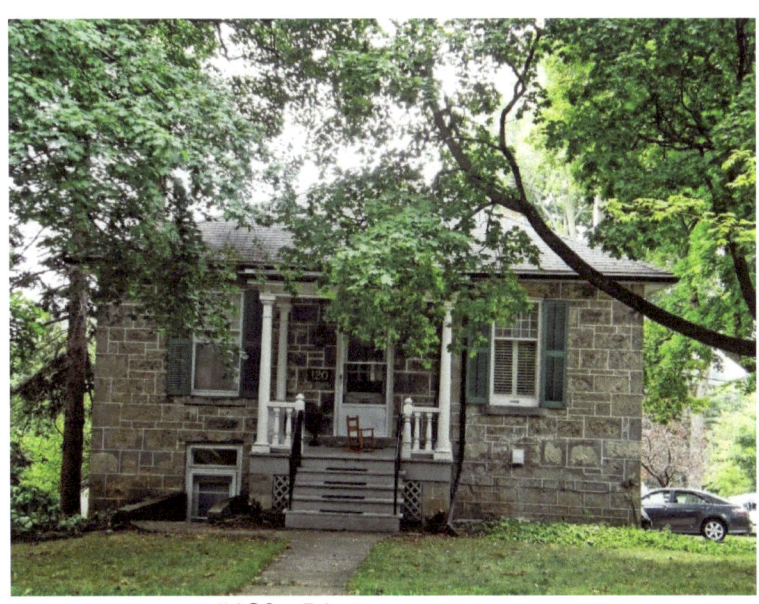

#120 - Limestone cottage

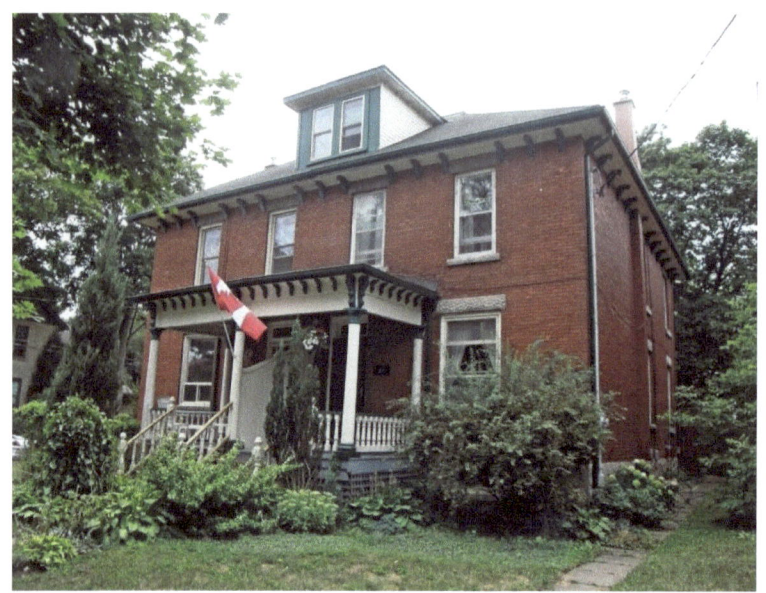

#64 – Italianate - red brick, dormer in attic, cornice brackets

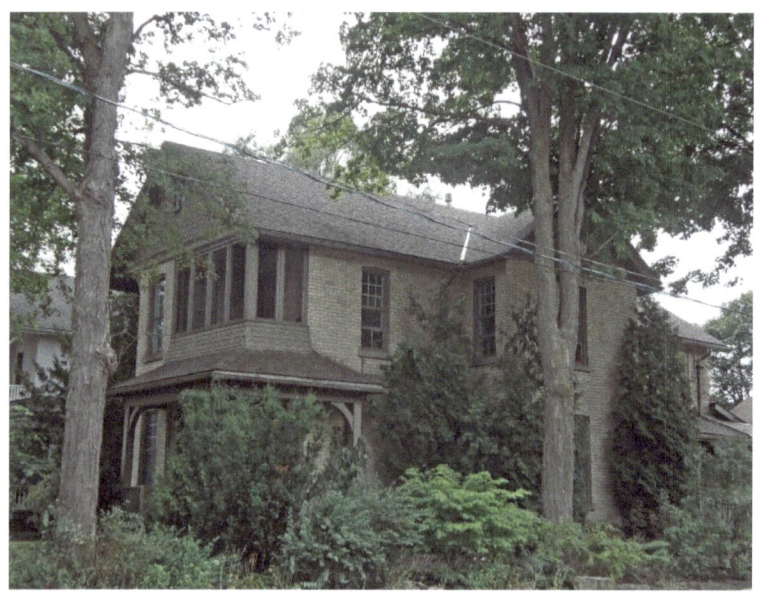

Gothic Revival - yellow brick

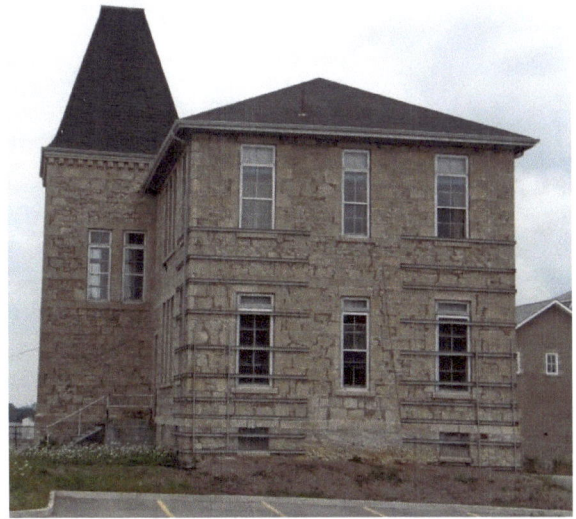

limestone

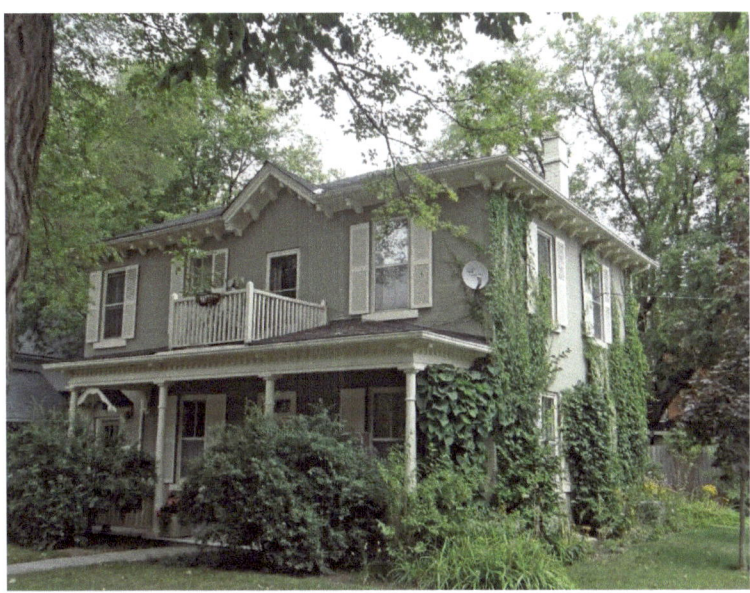

Italianate – cornice brackets, balcony on second floor

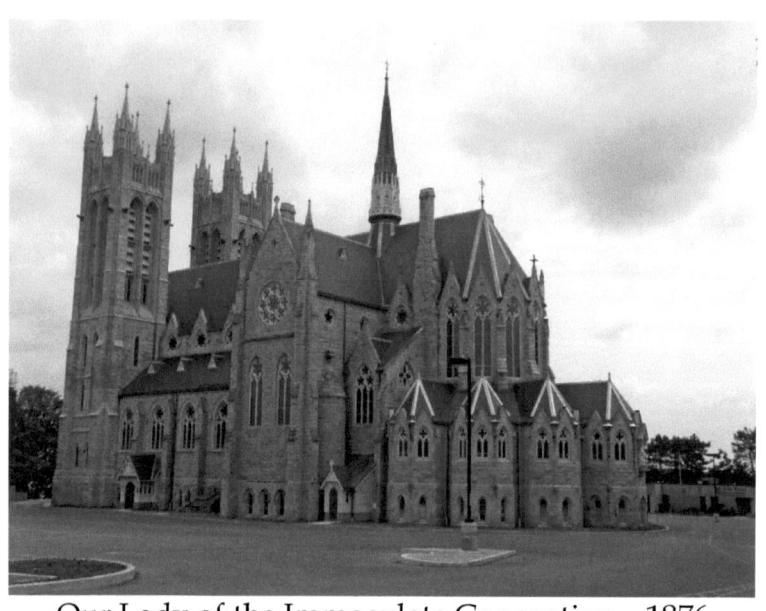

Our Lady of the Immaculate Conception – 1876
Thirteenth century French Gothic style

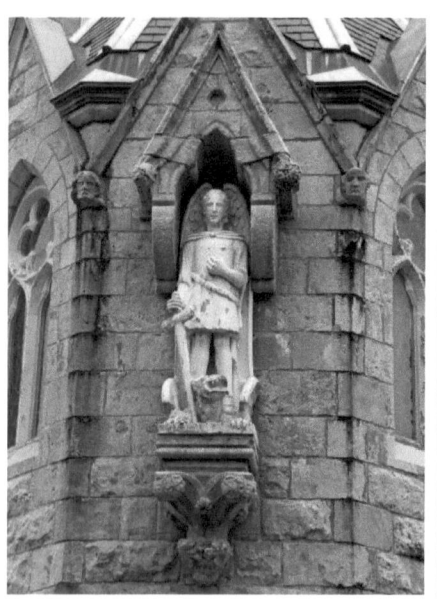

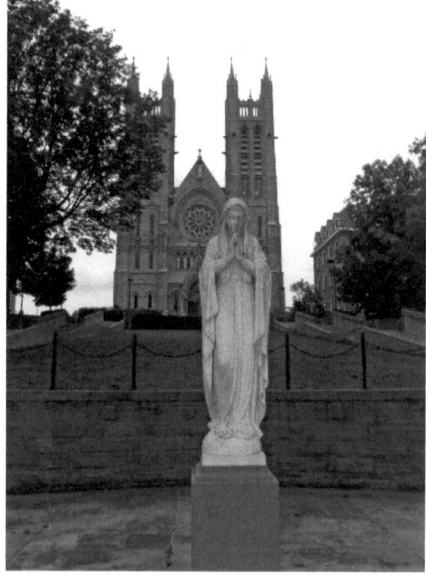

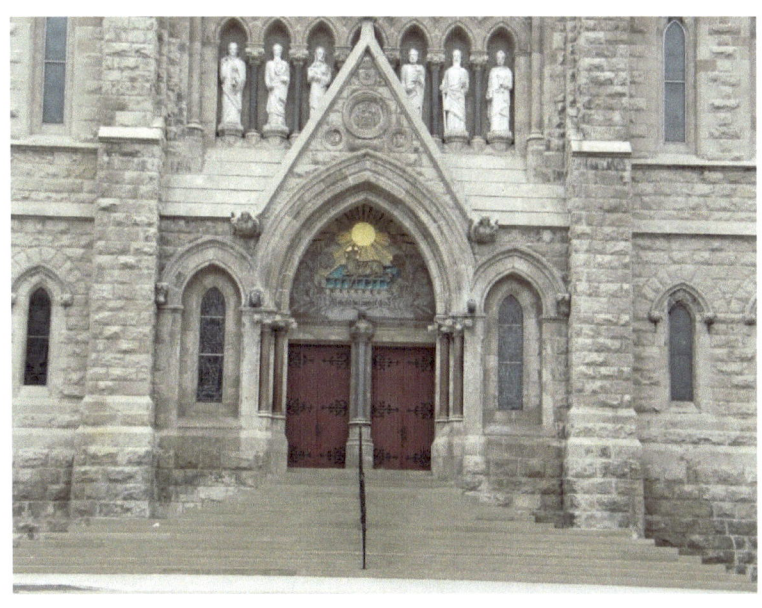

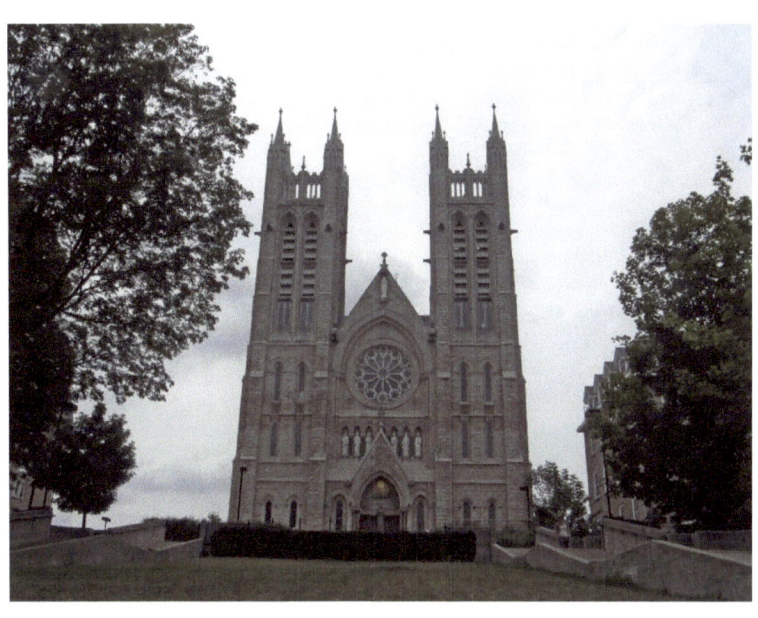

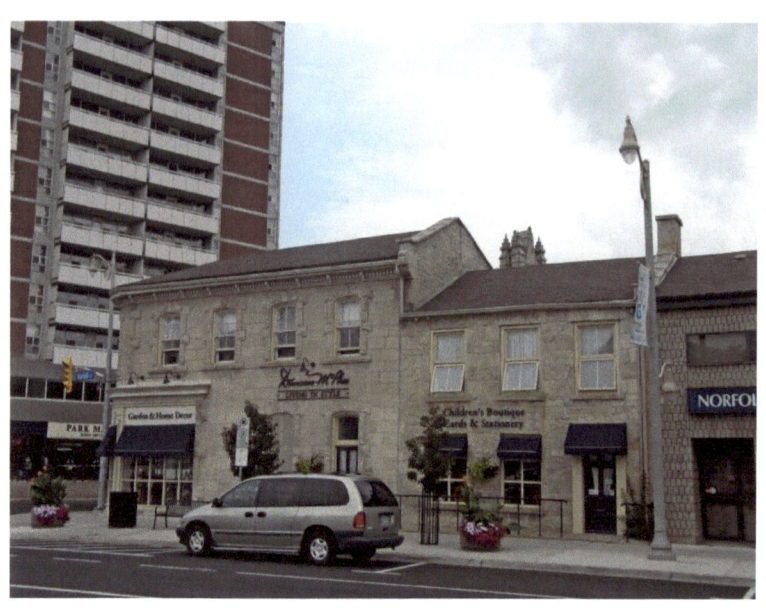

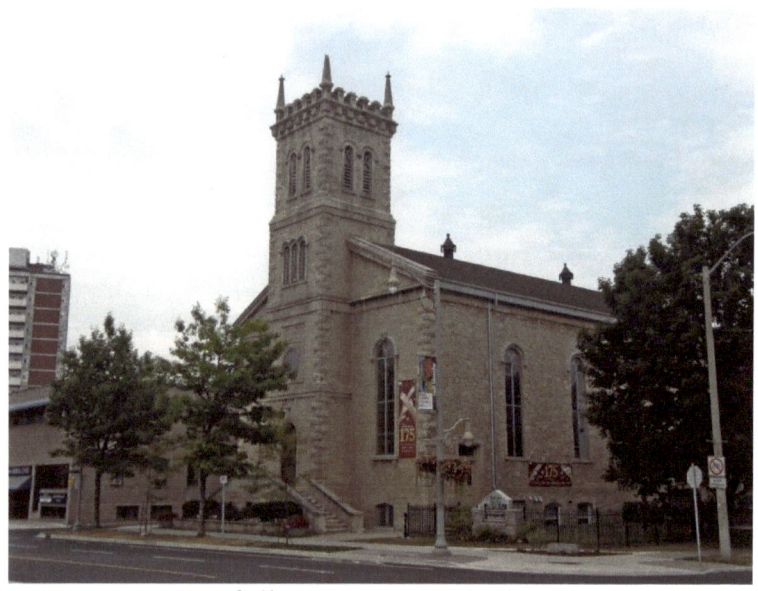

Norfolk Street United Church
1836-2011 – 175 years
(Wesleyan Methodist Church A.D. 1855)

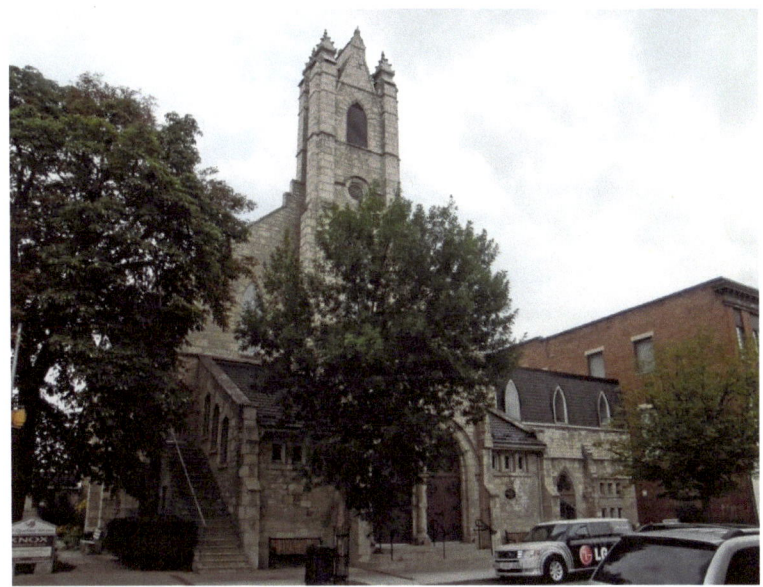

20 Quebec Street - Knox Presbyterian Church established 1844

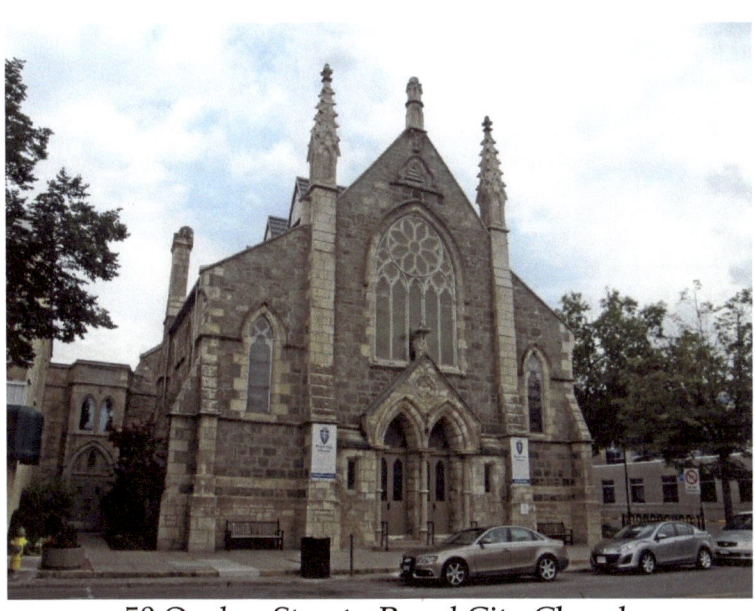

50 Quebec Street - Royal City Church

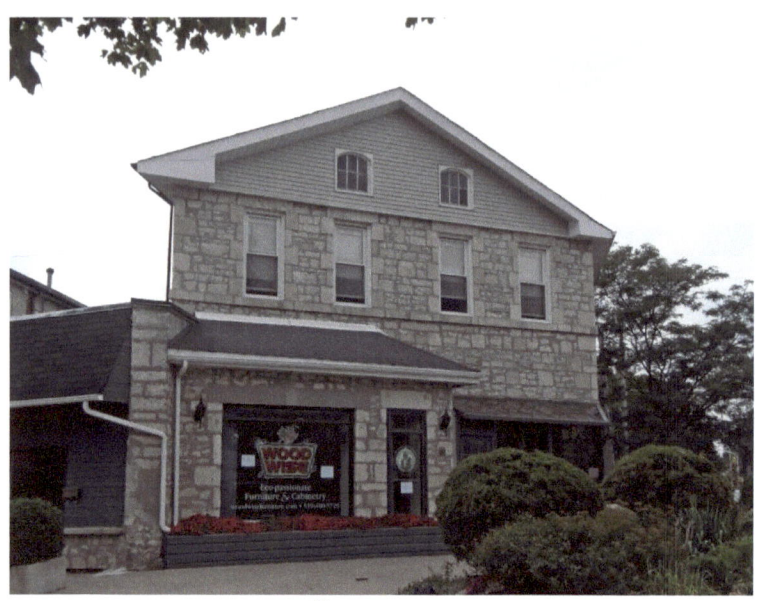

limestone

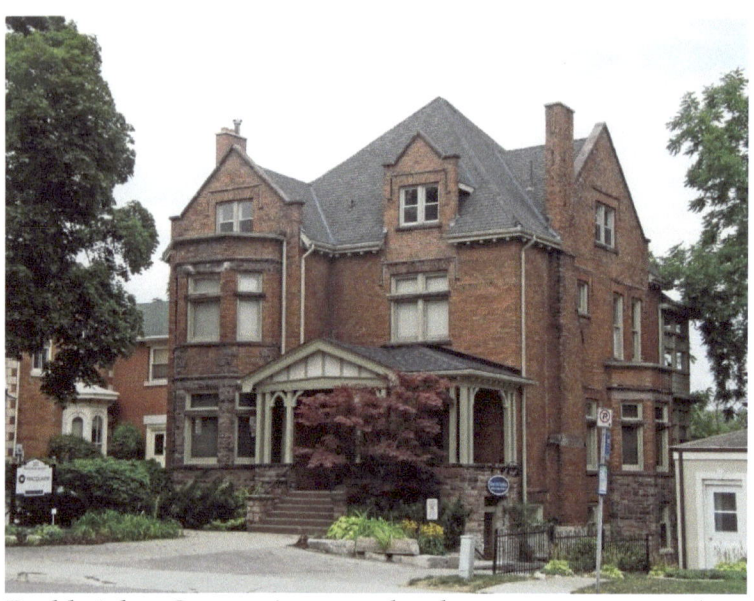

Red brick – Queen Anne style, three-storey tower, bay
window on side, pediment above verandah

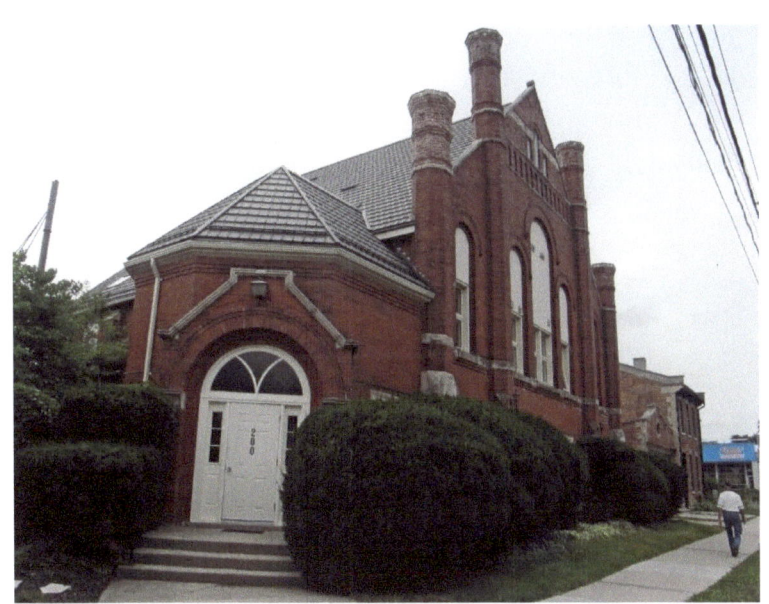

#200

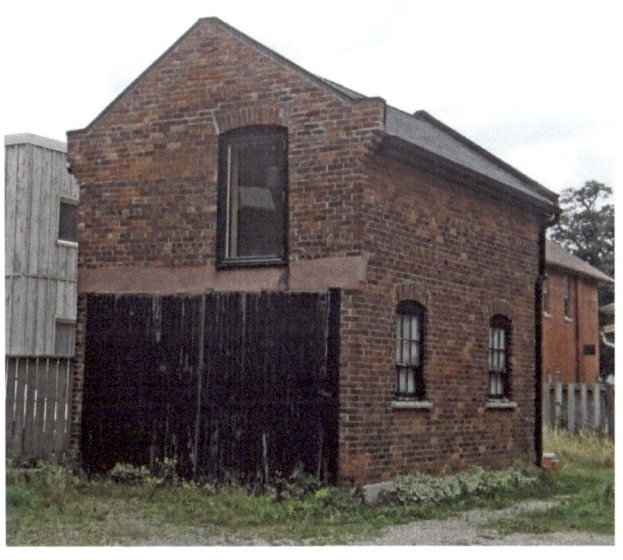

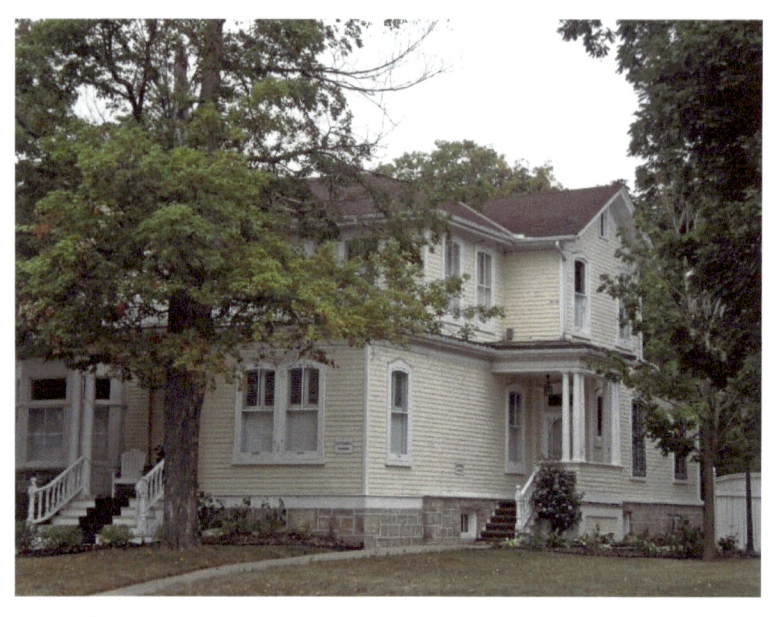

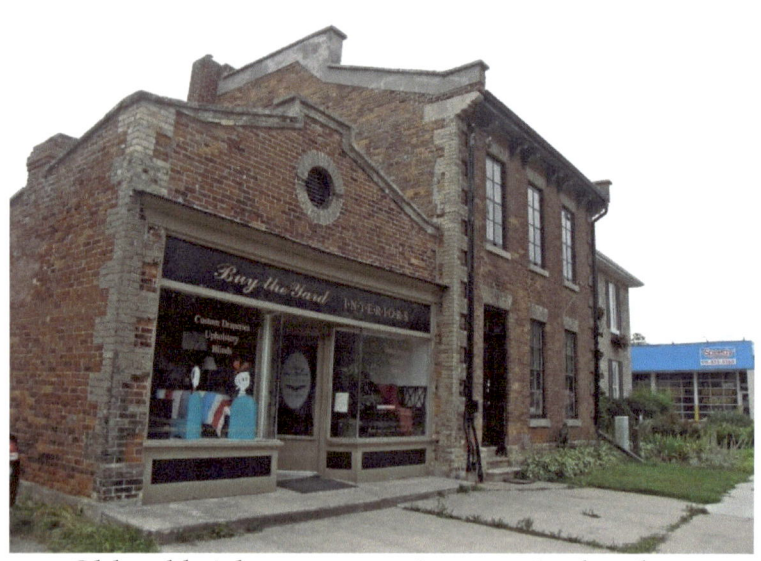

Old red brick, corner quoins, cornice brackets

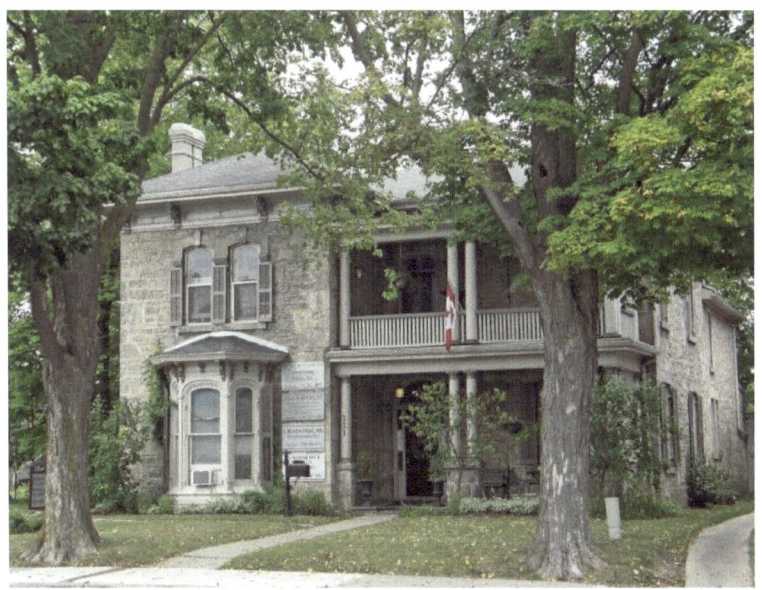

#221 – Italianate – hipped roof, limestone, bay window, arched lintels with keystones

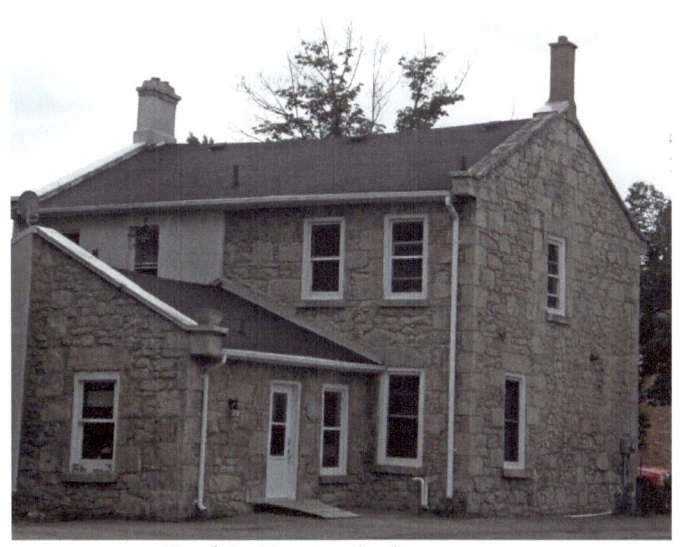

Gothic Revival - limestone

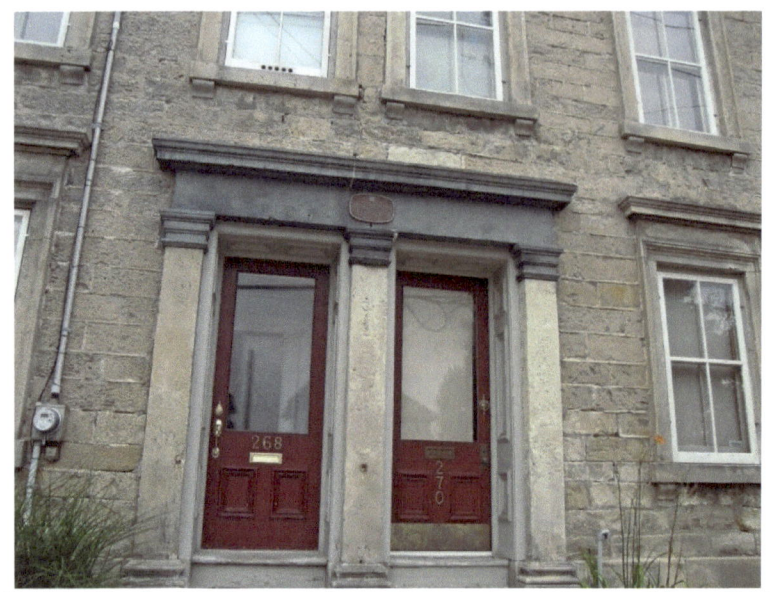

268-270 Woolwich Street – featuring characteristics of late 1840s, early 1850s such as bevelled corner quoins, stone cornice with carved eaves troughs, carved stone window details and entrance entablatures on monolithic stone pilasters

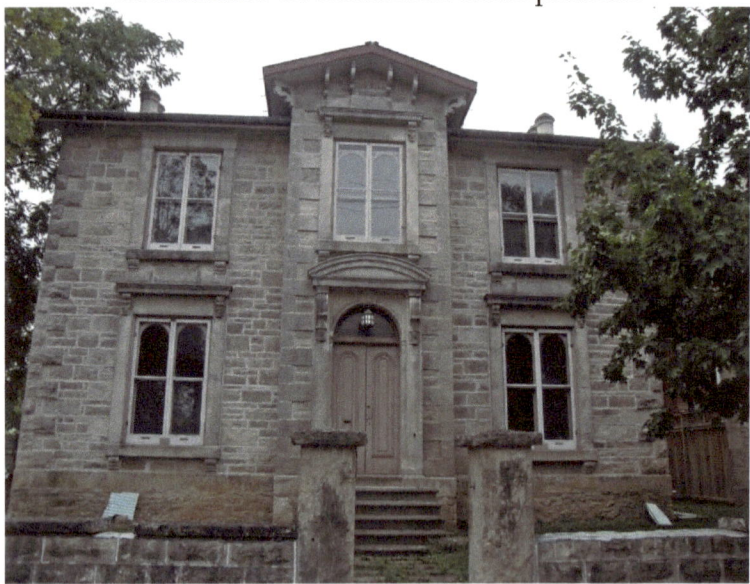

264 Woolwich Street displays the richly-carved Italianate ornamentation of the mid-19th century – in local limestone

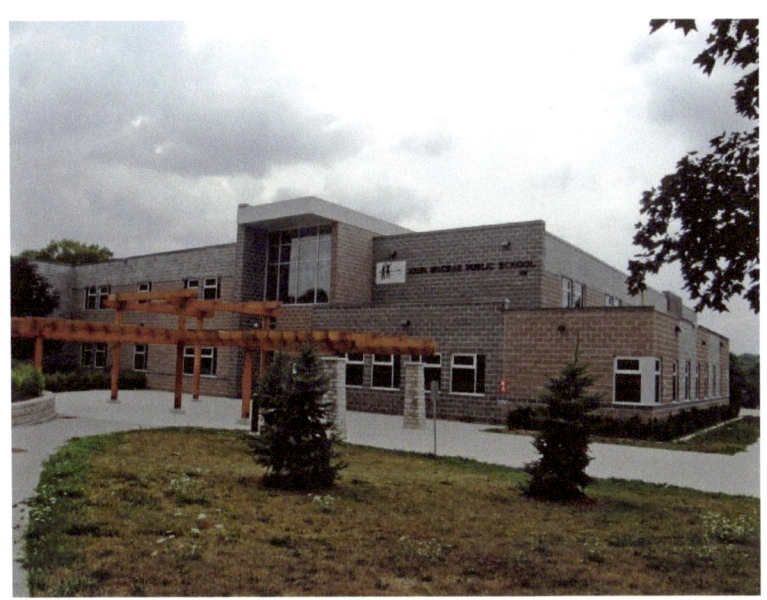

John McCrae Public School
where Grandma Todd was caretaker

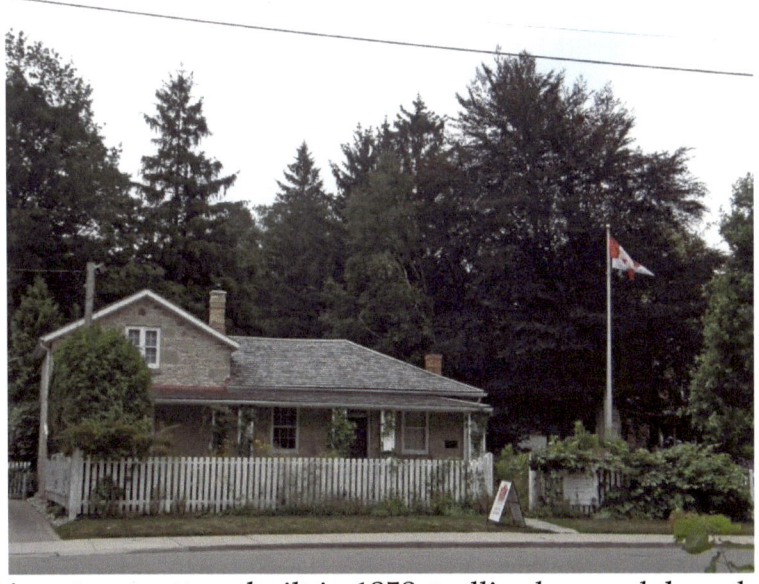

Limestone cottage built in 1858, trellised verandah, cedar
shingle roof - John McCrae born here on November 30, 1872
He wrote "In Flanders Fields"

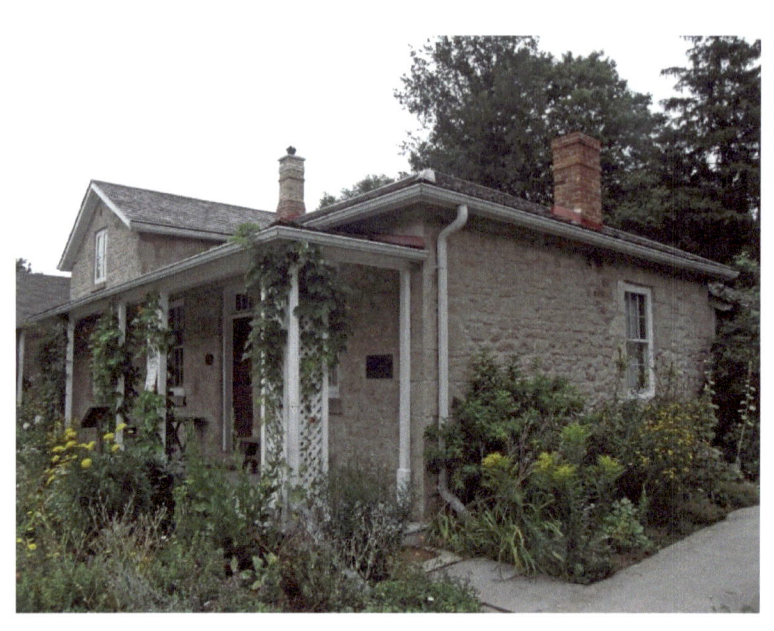

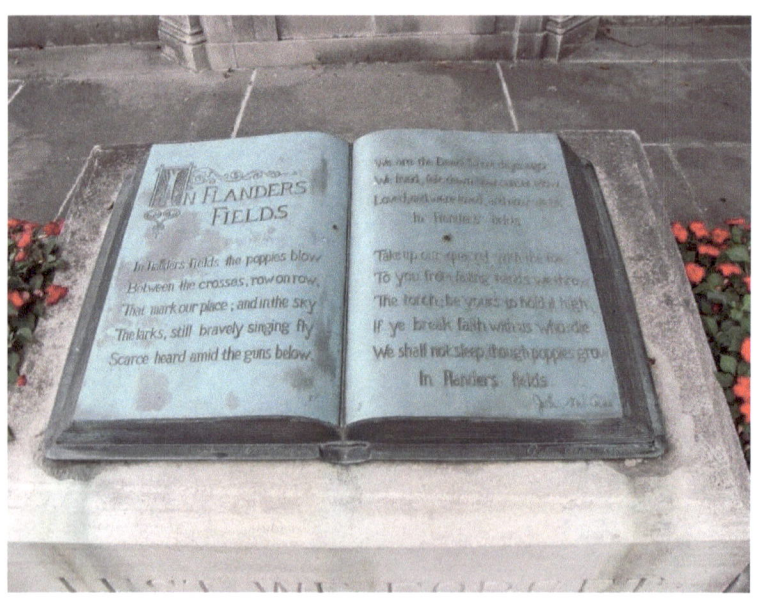

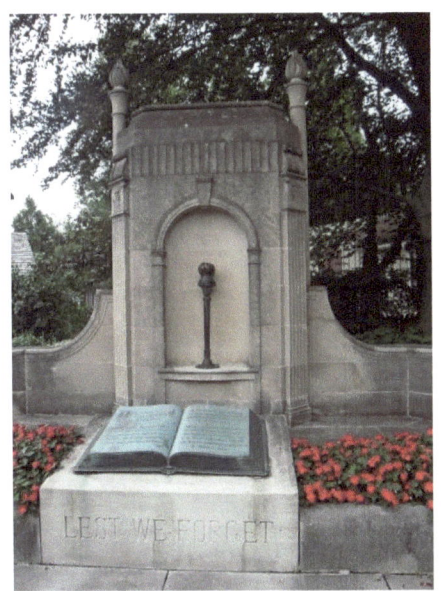

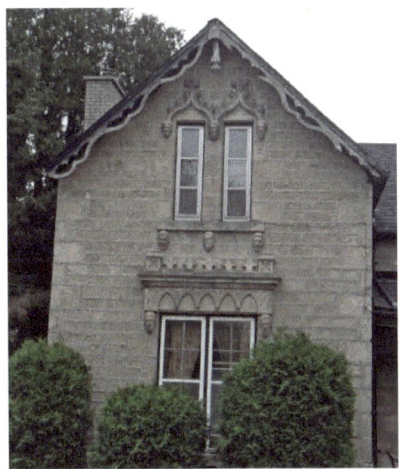

Verge board trim on gable with finial, heads in design, decorative window hoods

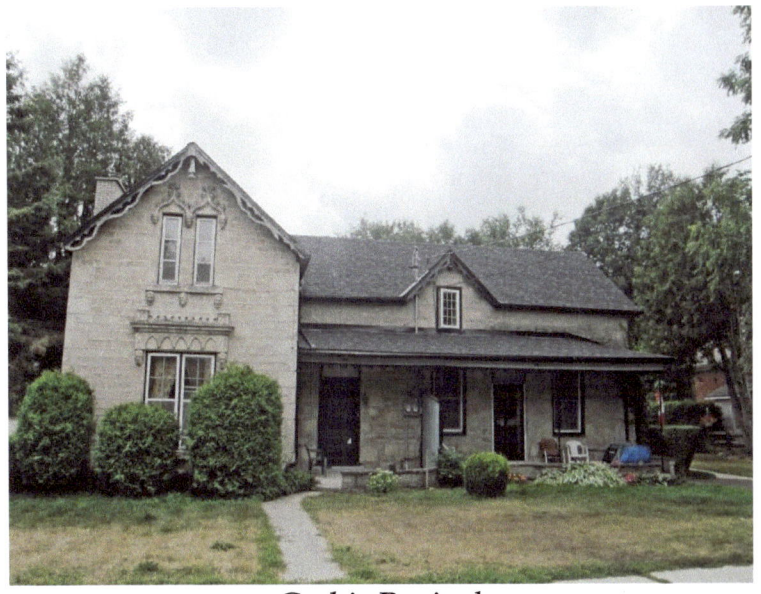

Gothic Revival

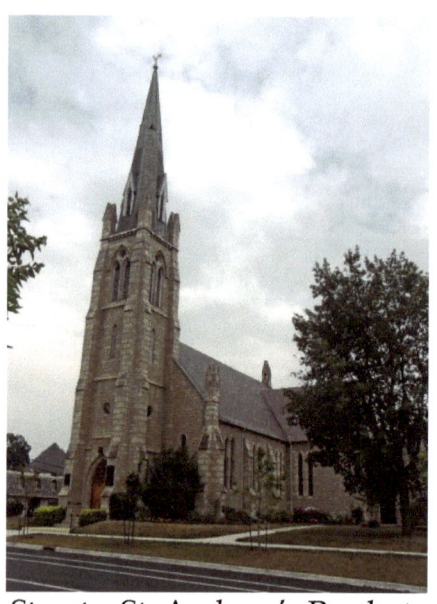

161 Norfolk Street – St. Andrew's Presbyterian Church

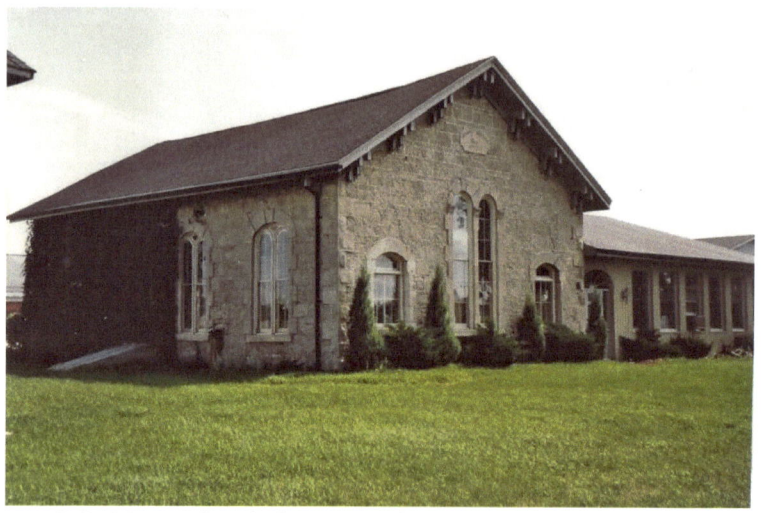

S.S. No. 1 Guelph Township School – A.D. 1873
Where I attended Grades 1 to 6 from 1957-63
Limestone, paired cornice brackets

University of Guelph

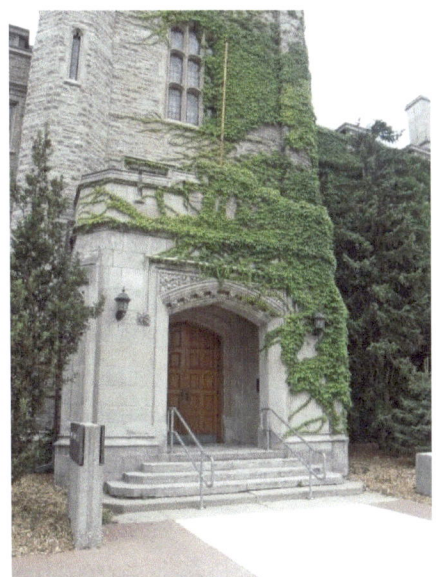

Johnston Hall built in 1932 as a student residence and administrative offices, named after the first principal

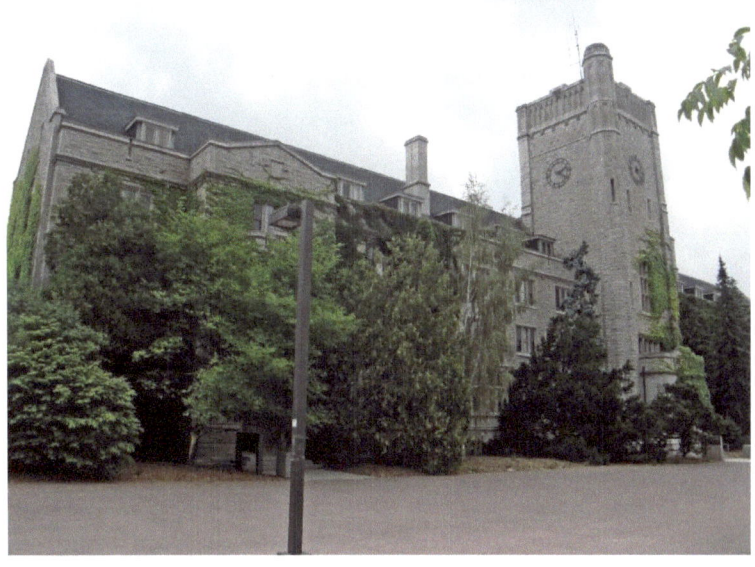

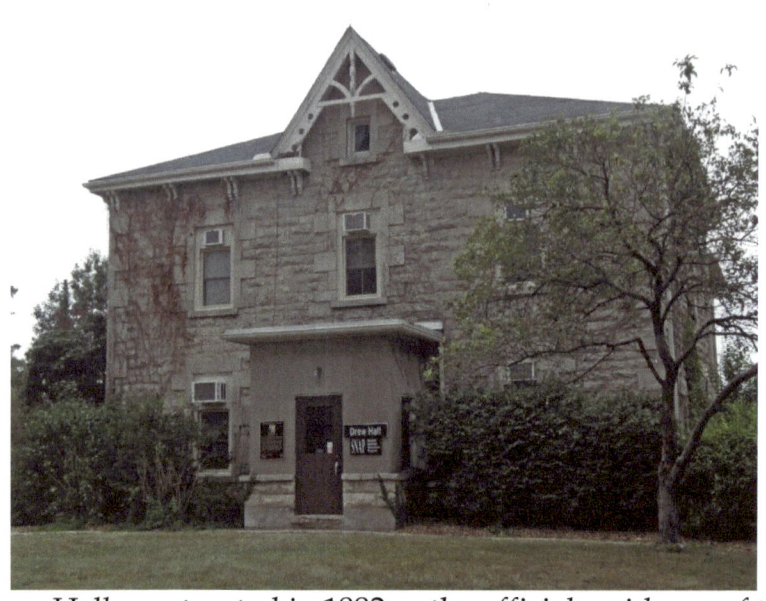

Drew Hall constructed in 1882 as the official residence of the Bursar, now used as offices for Hospitality Services

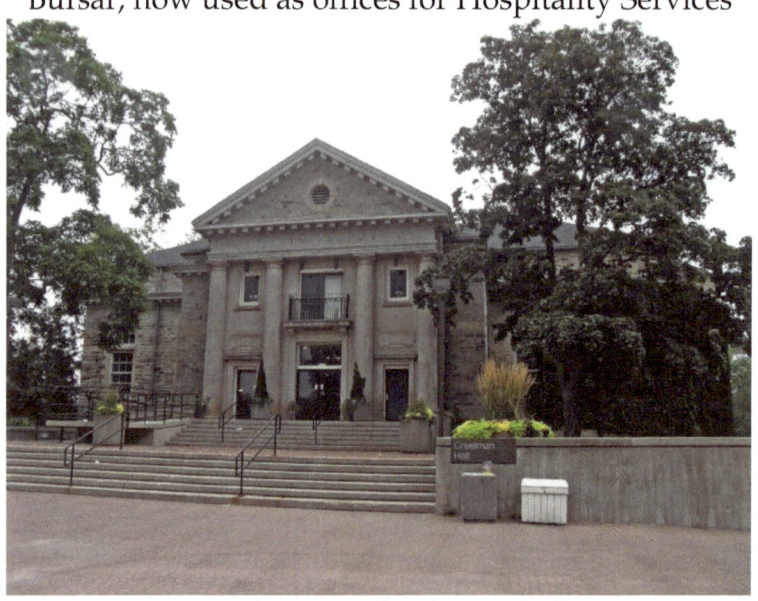

Creelman Hall – dining hall

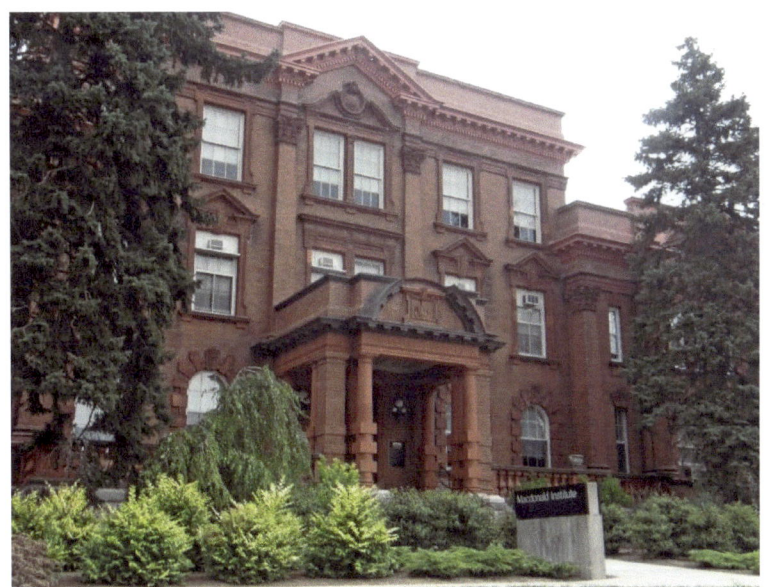

Opened in 1903, Macdonald Institute was co-founded by
Adelaide Hoodless and Sir William Macdonald, initially for
instruction for young women in nature study, manual
training, domestic science and domestic art

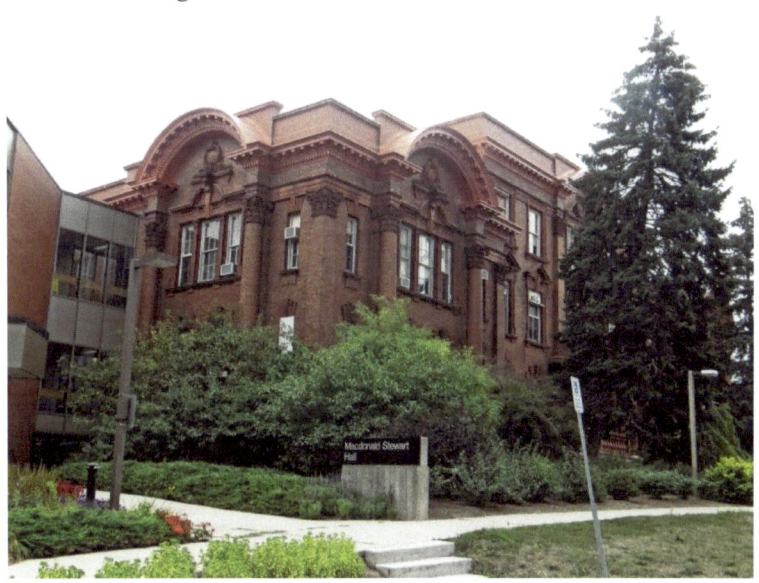

Macdonald Stewart Hall – residence

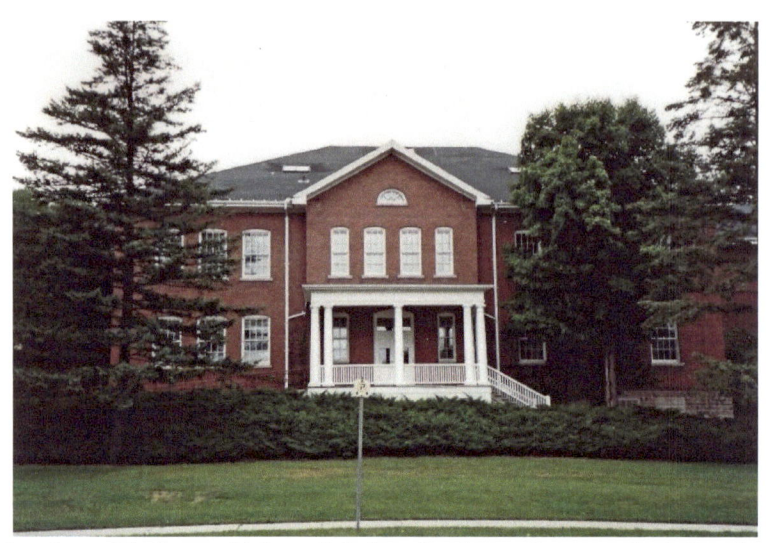

Macdonald Consolidated School where I attended Grade 7
– it closed in 1972 and reopened as
The Macdonald Stewart Art Institute

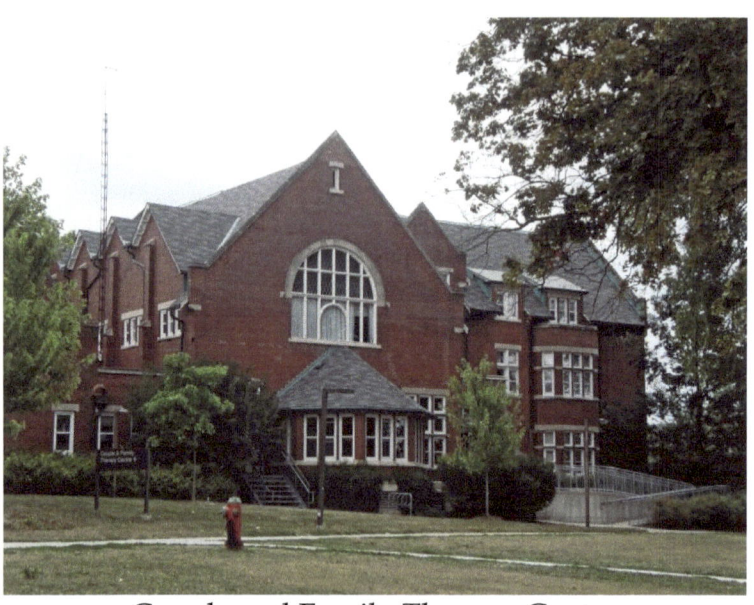

Couple and Family Therapy Centre

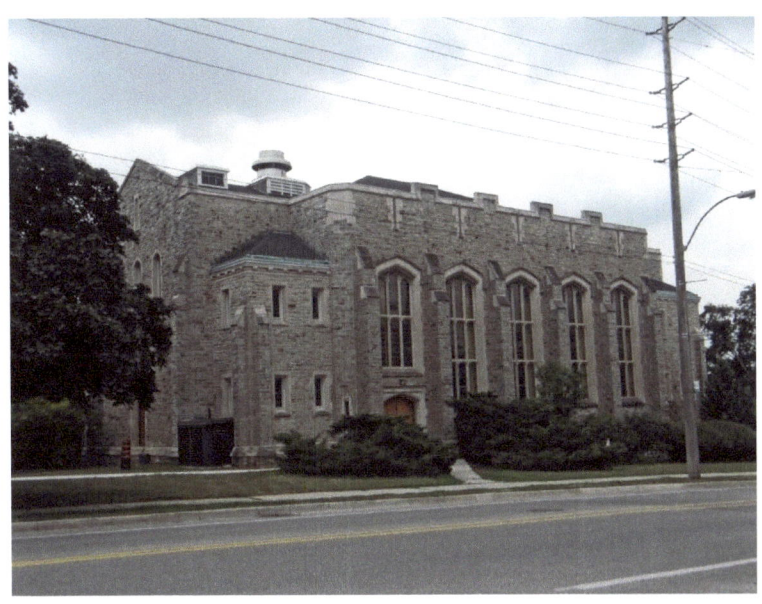

War Memorial Hall built in June 1924 as a lecture hall to honour students who had enlisted and died in World War I

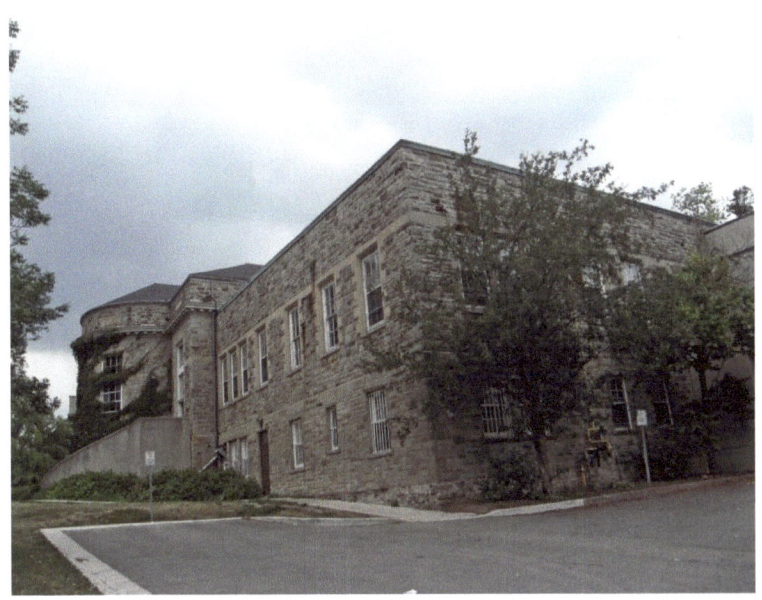

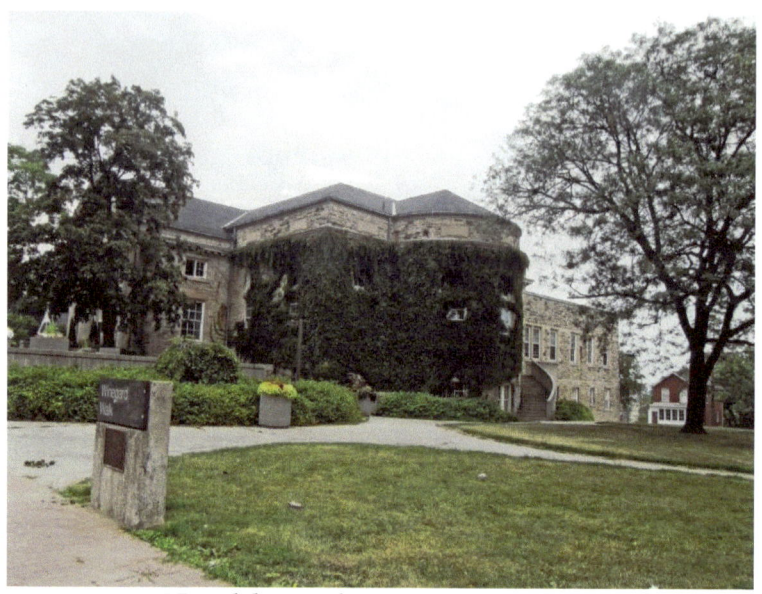

Hand-hewn limestone building

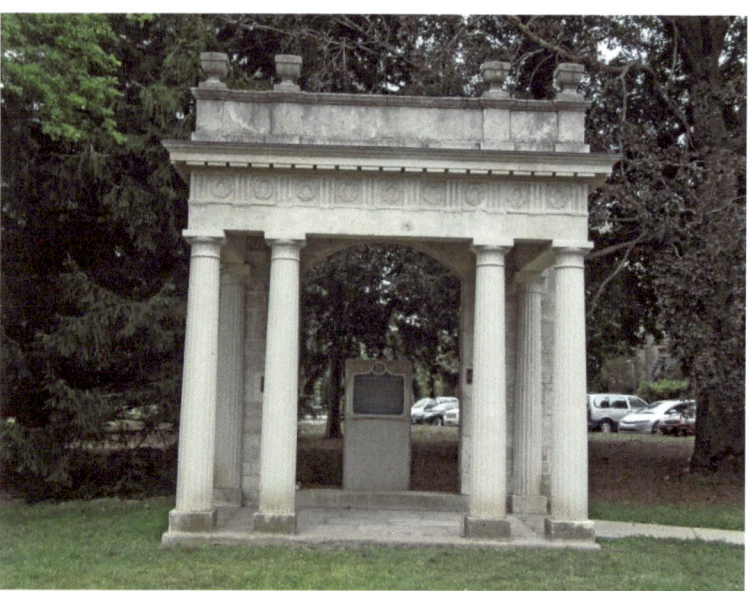

This portico was the entrance of the Frederick W. Stone farmhouse, the building in which the first classes of the Ontario School of Agriculture were held on May 1, 1874. 56 generations of students passed through this portal from 1874-1930.

Moffat

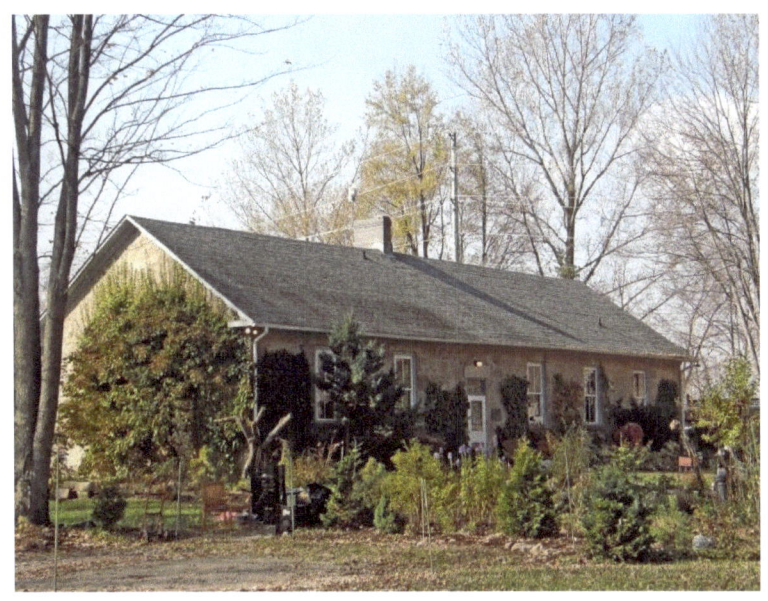

S.S. No. 3 School, Moffat – built in 1870

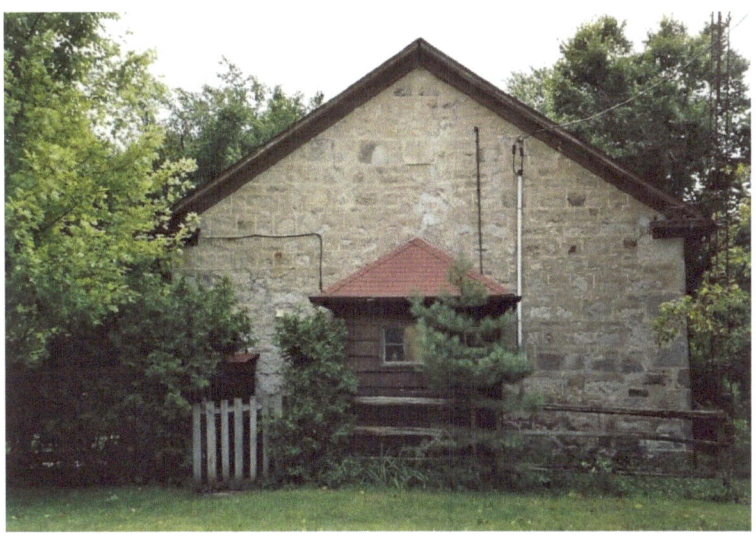

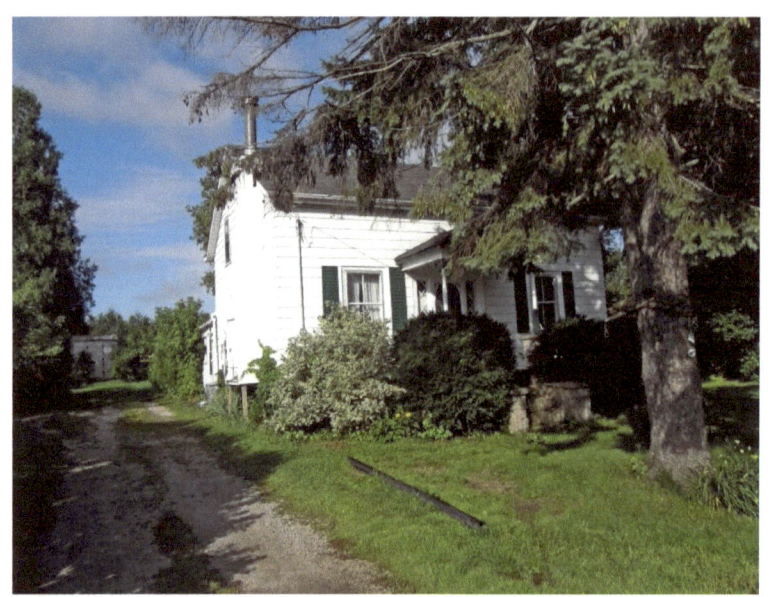

The house we lived in 1954-1956

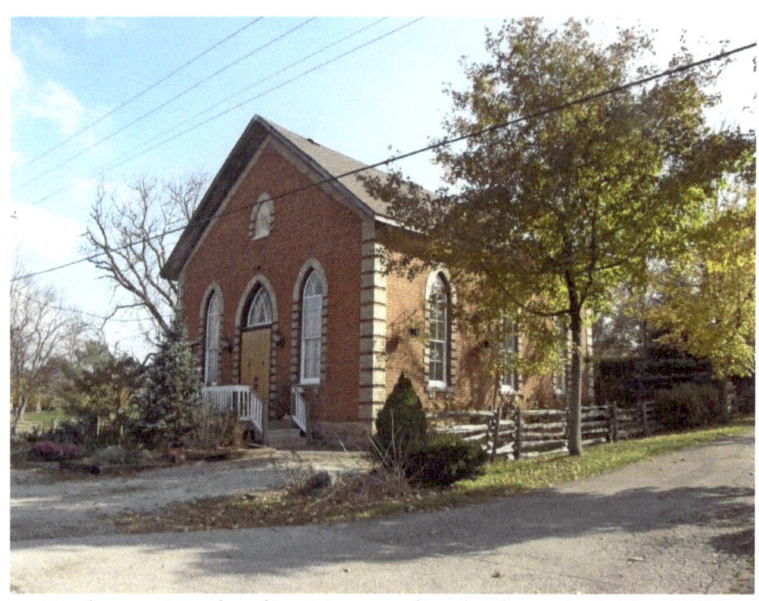

Bethany Methodist Evangelical Church A.D. 1877

Architectural Terms

Belvedere: (from the Italian "beautiful view") an architectural feature on a roof, in a garden or on a terrace that gives a beautiful view. Example:	
Brackets: a decorative or weight-bearing structural element which forms a right angle with one side against a wall and the other under a projecting surface such as an eave or roof. Example: see Page 20	
Buttress: a masonry structure built against or projecting from a wall which serves to support or reinforce the wall. In Canadian architecture, they are sometimes used for decoration. Example: 255 Woolwich Street (see Page 11)	
Cornice: originally the wooden overhang of the roof. With the use of stone, brick, iron and steel, the cornice is any projecting shelf at the top of a ceiling or roof. They can be very decorative. Example: see Page 26	
Cornice Return: decorative element on the end of a gable. Example: 258 Woolwich Street (see Page 11)	
Cupola: A domed or curved roof rising from a building as a decorative element. Example: 21 Stuart Street	
Dichromatic brickwork: the use of two colours of brick, tile or slate to decorate a façade. Example: see Page 14	

Dormer: (French for "sleep") a gable end window that pierces through the plane of a sloping roof surface to create usable space in the top floor or attic of a building by adding headroom. Example: see Page 5	
Entrance: The entrance encompasses the doorway and the inner vestibule or, in residential architecture, the covered porch. Example: see Page 22	
Gable: the triangular portion of a wall between the edges of a sloping roof. Example: see Page 24	
Hipped Roof: a roof where all sides slope downwards to the walls with no gables. Example: see Page 20	
Iron Cresting: A decorative ornament along the top of a roof. Iron cresting was popular in the Baroque era and also in Italianate, Victorian, Second Empire and Queen Anne styles of architecture. Example: 143 Norfolk Street	
Keystone: the central stone that locks all the stones into position, allowing the arch to bear weight. A keystone is often enlarged and embellished. Example: see Page 20	
Lancet Window: a tall, narrow window with a pointed arch at its top. Example: 255 Woolwich Street, First Baptist Church	

Palladian Window: a large window that is divided into three sections with the centre section larger than the two side sections and usually arched. Example: see Page 15	
Pediment: a triangular section above the horizontal structure (entablature), typically supported by columns. The inside of the triangle is called the tympanum. Example: see Page 32	
Pilaster: a slightly projecting column built into or applied to the face of a wall for additional structural support. Example: 268-270 Woolwich Street	
Quoin: masonry blocks at the corner of a wall, often a decorative feature, usually larger or of a different colour than the rest of the wall. Example: see Page 22	
Rose Window: a circular window with ornamental tracery radiating from the centre. Example: Our Lady of the Immaculate Conception Church	

Vergeboard and Finial: also called bargeboards – hang from the projecting end of a roof and are often elaborately carved and ornamented. **Finial:** ornament added to the top of a gable, pinnacle, canopy or spire – a Gothic element. Example: see Page 39	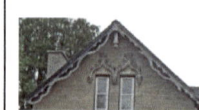
Window Hood: A **hood** is the piece found above window openings, usually of an ornate design, and covers the top third of the opening. Hoods are commonly placed above arched or curved openings on both windows and doors. Example: see Page 22	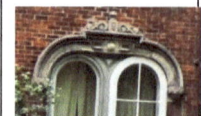

Building Styles

Edwardian, 1900-1930 – This style bridges the ornate and elaborate styles of the Victorian era and the simplified styles of the 20th century. Balanced facades, simple roof lines, dormer windows, large front porches, and smooth brick surfaces are its characteristics. Example: see Page 17	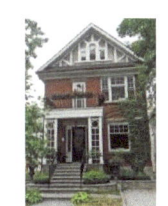
Georgian, before 1860 – This style began with the British King Georges in the 18th century. These buildings have balanced facades around a central door, medium-pitched gable roofs, and small paned windows. Example: 21 Stuart Street	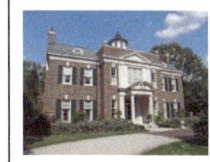
Gothic Revival, 1830-1890 – These decorative buildings have sharply-pitched gables with highly detailed verge boards, pointed-arch window openings, and dichromatic brickwork. It is a common style in Ontario. Example: see Page 39	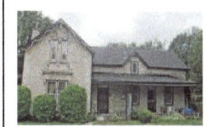
Italianate, 1850-1900 – It has wide-bracketed eaves, belvederes, wrap-around verandahs. Example: see Page 21	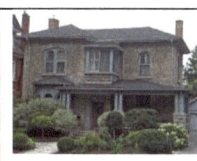

Queen Anne, 1885-1900 – This style is distinguished by an irregular outline featuring a combination of an offset tower, broad gables, projecting two-storey bays, verandahs, multi-sloped roofs, and tall, decorative chimneys. A mixture of brick and wood is common. Windows often have one large single-paned bottom sash and small panes in the upper sash. Example: see Page 32	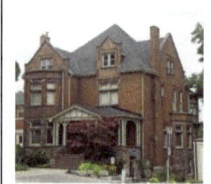
Tudor Revival – exposed timbers with stucco infill, multi-paned windows. Example: see Page 9	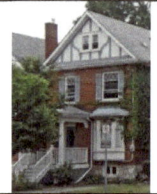